RUMOR IN THE MARKETPLACE

RUMOR IN THE MARKETPLACE

The Social Psychology of Commercial Hearsay

Fredrick Koenig
Tulane University

 Auburn House Publishing Company
Dover, Massachusetts • London

89119

*This book is dedicated to my parents,
Ernest Koenig and Laura Koenig, who
introduced me to the world of books.*

Library of Congress Cataloging in Publication Data

Koenig, Fredrick W.
  Rumor in the market place.

  Bibliography: p.
  Includes index.
  1. Corporate image.   2. Rumor.   3. Social psychology.
I. Title.
HD59.2.K63 1984   302.2′4   84-12379
ISBN 0-86569-117-7

FOREWORD

Who steals my purse steals trash.
But he who filches from me my good name
Robs me of that which not enriches him
And makes me poor indeed.
                    —William Shakespeare

This book contains some of the wildest stories you ever heard: Spider eggs in chewing gum; underwear rendering men sterile; earthworms in hamburgers. And perhaps most bizarre of all, allegations that a $13 billion company (which takes infinite pains to see that the public perceives it as being as pure as driven Ivory Snow) is in league with the Devil.

Lies, every one of them! Yet tens upon thousands of people have believed—or repeated—these and many other false and malicious rumors, causing anguish and pain to some of the nation's leading companies and damaging their good corporate names.

That is the frightening thing about commercial rumors; they are no less dangerous for being totally absurd and patently preposterous. Unsquelched, a rampaging rumor can erode a product's sales, damage its market share, and even put workers out of their jobs. Failure to convince the public that a rumor is without a grain of truth can damage a company's relations with its customers and suppliers and cause stockholders to question management's ability to deal responsibly with a monstrous problem.

Indeed, next to an act of terrorism, what corporations fear most is that they may be targeted with an outlandish tall tale. Many large companies have drawn up contingency plans and procedures against the day it happens to them. Unhappily, most others have not, for the simple reason that so little is known about coping with rumors that the methodology is far from empirical. As a public relations executive of a major food company once told me after a nasty experience with rumormongers, "I've been in this business twenty years and I've never seen anything like it. Squelching a rumor is like trying to package fog."

But now there is light. In *Rumor in the Marketplace*, Fredrick Koenig has assembled just about every major rumor that has surfaced in recent years to plague corporations. A foremost authority on commercial rumors, he not only analyzes their origins and details the courses companies have followed to stifle them but outlines a sensible program for dealing with them deftly, swiftly, and effectively. A PR man I know claims that he keeps Koenig's rules for refuting rumors framed on his office wall and looks at them all the time.

I first encountered Fred Koenig in 1981 while researching an article on commercial rumors for *Dun's Business Month.* It was not enough merely to report current rumors and to describe what companies were doing about them; I needed an expert who could provide insights into the anatomy of rumors—how do they get started, who spreads them and why? The sources I checked were unanimous: Talk to Fred Koenig at Tulane.

I soon discovered that the genial professor of social psychology, who serves as a consultant to corporations with rumor problems, has amassed comprehensive files on the subject. His input to my story, "Tilting at the Rumor Mill," was invaluable.

Two years in the writing, *Rumor in the Marketplace* is the first book to probe this potentially devastating problem. It ought to be required reading for corporate decisionmakers everywhere.

Robert Levy
Senior Editor, *Dun's Business Month*

PREFACE

Today rumors are a compelling topic of study and discussion by both business people and academics. But this was not always true. Not many years ago, rumors were studied as a part of social psychology known as collective behavior—a delicious, puffy meringue portion compared with the solid substantial protein offerings involving controlled, carefully measured research. Gustave LeBon watched the mobs rioting in Paris in the late 19th century and tried to make sense of it all by positing such ideas as group mind, social contagion, and the like. Not very solid stuff scientifically, but fascinating to many. His book *The Crowd* was a prototype for the early collective behavior side of social psychology.

At the same time, on the other side of the discipline, Norman Triplett noticed that bicycle riders went faster when racing with others than when timed alone. In an experiment using children winding fishing reels alone or in groups, he carefully measured the differences in speed in each condition. This exercise was an early experiment in social psychology on dynamogenesis, later called social facilitation. To me there is no question about which work— LeBon's or Triplett's—was initially more interesting and which was more scientific. When I took my first course in social psychology in the late forties, however, collective behavior was still a major component of social psychology. I remember getting my G.I. Bill bag of books and digging out the two on social psychology. I started reading one of them on the streetcar and kept on after reaching home. This material on collective behavior was fascinating stuff, describing epidemics of crazed behavior sweeping across nations: emotional outbreaks in church, a frightening (but non-existent) Mattoon anesthetist terrorizing a town by sneaking up on women with his potion, panic resulting from a radio drama about a Martian invasion, and rumors—rumors of impending earthquakes, rumors of atrocity killings, rumors of racial turmoil, rumors of political cover-ups of waste and tragedy. In my final college year I took a course in which an entire semester was devoted to collective behavior. It subsequently became apparent to most people involved, however, that not enough was known scientifically about the topic to warrant a place for it in the curriculum, and it was phased rapidly out of the social psychology scene.

Rumor was more fortunate than collective behavior and many other topics in that it had an early scientific tradition associated with Gordon Allport's experiments with "telephone" as a model of rumor transmission. Other aspects of rumor also proved amenable to experiments, helping to keep rumor a somewhat respectable interest in social psychology.

As will be evident in this book, I sensed a new turn in rumors: more and more were about products, producers, corporations, and retailers. It seemed to me that much of this new wave could be tied to the emerging approach of producing and merchandising through huge corporations and nation-wide franchises, turning our society into one large, homogenous marketplace. This development, along with the propensity of the mass media—especially television—to bombard the population with messages involving the logos, slogans, and attributes of products, producers, corporations, and retailers, made everyone familiar with companies as a shared experience of corporate presence in their lives. Consequently, these commercial entities became recognizable all over the country and thereby acquired vulnerability as targets of allegations and rumors—with nation-wide implications.

Actually, the commercial rumor is not entirely new. A few versions were kicking around in the 1930s. For example, there was a contamination rumor that Chesterfield cigarettes were made in a factory that employed a leper and a conspiracy rumor that the Camel cigarettes company was connected with the Vatican. There were contamination rumors about certain soft drinks containing this or that undesirable ingredient, including a mouse in a bottle. At that time, such stories were scattered and low key. In the late 1970s, however, they became the dominant form of rumor. Even traditional sources of hearsay, such as racial conflict, became manifested in the current format: Fears that whites had about blacks were expressed in a Stroh's Beer rumor, and fears that blacks had about whites were expressed in a rumor about Church's Fried Chicken. (Both of these rumors are discussed in this book.) In short, commercial rumor, because of its unique variations from previous, traditional genres, deserves special attention as a topic for a book, hence the writing of these chapters.

In going the long trail from pencil sharpener to publication, I would like to acknowledge assistance from the following people:

> Jim Asker, The Houston Post Company
> R. Sue Denny, The Stroh Brewery Company
> Frank Dobisky, Dobisky Associates
> William Dobson, The Procter & Gamble Company
> Trécie Fennell, General Food Corporation
> Hal Goodman, *Across the Board*
> Mel Grayson, Squib Corporation
> William Herman, Jockey International, Inc.
> Jack Levin, Northeastern University
> Lottie Lindberg, *The Wall Street Journal*
> Susan McKelvey, K mart Inc.
> Roger Nunley, The Coca-Cola Company
> Ken Ross, Pepsico
> Doug Timberlake, Weber, Cohn and Riley
> Larry Varney, Grey Advertising Agency
> Walter Weglein, Warner-Lambert Company

I would like to offer special appreciation to the following people:

> Professor Edward V. Morse, who, as my department chairman, went out of his way to provide me with extra equipment, facilities, and space.
> Gwendolyn Marionita Williams and Jane Tamae Kuroda, who waded through tons of pages of illegible handwriting and circuitous, pasted revisions to come up with clean copy time and again.
> Dorothy Whittemore and Eleanore D. Merritt, librarians at the Norman Meyer Library of Tulane's School of Business, who helped me find corporate phone numbers and back issues of various business publications.
> Meredith Meyers, an opportune daughter who kept me current with rumors of the young set.

And, last of all, I acknowledge the seeming hordes of colleagues, friends, and acquaintances who drove me to ever higher pinnacles of motivation with their constant, "I thought you said you were coming out with a book!"

F.K.

CONTENTS

CHAPTER 9

CHAPTER 10

Chapter One

INTRODUCTION

Several years ago while attending a convention in Washington, D.C., I received a phone call from Jan White of the Associated Press in New York. "Have you heard the rumor about Procter & Gamble?" she asked. "It tells how they are connected to a satanic witchcraft cult." I had indeed seen a story on this subject in the *Washington Post* the day before and noted it with interest. During the previous year, I had worked with people at McDonald's Corporation on a similar rumor concerning *their* supposed connection with the Church of Satan.[1]

Although I have been involved in various aspects of social psychology for over three decades, I have never worked with any topic that attracts as much attention as does rumor. It is a phenomenon that we have all experienced in one fashion or another, yet it has an anomalous character. We have become aware of its intriguing qualities, its destructive power, its illusiveness and mystery of origin. Because of this general interest, media people find rumors "good copy." Jan White was no exception, and she had questions about the Procter & Gamble story such as, "Who starts these rumors?" (we don't know) and "What can be done to stop them?" (it all depends). These are the questions most frequently posed, and therein lies one reason for writing this book. First, it is hard to say how rumors actually start or how to stop them. My sparse responses are correct as far as they go, but a single sentence cannot properly address the complexities involved. Tracing a rumor to a specific origin or originator is not usually a realistic task. Think of the last joke someone told you: Would it be feasible to work your way back to the person who originally made it up? Rumor is a similar form of communication, and it is more appropriate to think of these types of messages as *evolving* rather than as having specific beginnings.

Remedies for rumor vary, too, just as they do for headaches. They depend on the type and severity of the rumor and on the medical history and attitude of the patient; there is no single cure. In short, the rumor process is never a simple matter in its beginnings, endings, or at any stage in between. This book will examine some of the intricacies.

Some Definitions

Webster[2] gives a definition of rumor which is professionally acceptable and workable: A story or report current within any known authority for its truth. Ralph Rosnow,[3] a psychologist who has written extensively on the topic, defines rumor as "a proposition that is unverified and in general circulation." The fact that the information is unverified is important. Being unverified is not the same as being untrue. A rumor may turn out to be "true," but until it is verified it is subject to the dynamics of rumor. When it is verified, it is subject to the limitations presented by the facts. Much of the work on rumor assumes that the communication is interpersonal and by word of mouth, but this is not necessarily so, as we will see later.

The phenomenon of gossip is often linked to rumor. Although there are many similarities, it may be well to make some distinctions. For our present purposes I would like to delimit gossip as communication about people known to the persons involved in the communicating. Also gossip can be a bit of information that is verifiable, as when someone spends the weekend in jail, gets pregnant, or deserts a spouse. Although gossip and rumor may both be forms of diversion, gossip is a form of social control and a means of reinforcing group norms, in that people are motivated to conform in order to avoid being a target of gossip. Also people engage in gossip to establish their own respectability by implicitly comparing their own behavior favorably with that of the subject of the message. Those communicating disapproval of a behavior are emphasizing the importance of the norms being violated. The function of rumor, on the other hand, is usually other than the above, and that function will be a topic receiving special attention later on in this book.

Historical Background of Rumor Studies

The public and the press have been intrigued by rumor for a long time, but it has also been a topic for serious analysis by scholars. Virgil[4] refers to it in the *Aeneid* when he says, "Rumor, thou than which no other evil is swifter, thrives on movement and she gathers strength as she goes."

At the turn of the century, when scientific methods were applied to the study of human behavior, rumor became an object of scrutiny for sociologists, psychologists, psychiatrists, anthropologists, and folklorists. Most of the traditional studies have been oriented toward what I call the three *C*'s—crisis, conflict, and catastrophe. Rumors thrive under conditions of social trauma and personal threat and are often associated with major disturbing situations. Many rumors are associated with wars, minority group antagonism, economic and political crises, and natural disasters.

There are several noteworthy books which follow rumor analysis in this manner. Tomatso Shibutani's[5] book *Improvised News* lists 60 documented rumors, 38 of which are related to war and group conflicts, 13 to catastrophe, and 8 to social and personal crises. (There is one extraneous tale that deals with a miracle.) Rosnow and Fine's[6] *Rumor and Gossip* includes accounts of deaths of celebrities, racial rumors, wartime rumors, and rumors linked to catastrophes. Terry Knopf's[7] *Rumors, Race and Riots* and Howard Odum's[8] *Race and Rumors of Race* are what their titles imply. The first and most influential book in this field, *The Psychology of Rumor*, by Allport and Postman,[9] was clearly motivated by concerns stemming from World War II and the problems of race relations attendant to it.

The Legacy of Early Approaches

Scientific generalizations must be based on observations of events in a given setting. Social psychologists have always faced problems in studying collective behavior scientifically. Rumors, like most other forms of collective behavior, take place in a specialized social context, and they usually can be studied only as they occur. The situation is much like that of a meteorologist studying rainstorms in that rumors happen in "natural" systems as opposed to "constructed" systems (that is, in the real world rather than in a laboratory). As such they cannot be manipulated but can be observed only when they appear. Unlike marriages and other social events, however, they occur relatively infrequently; thus, there are very few events which can be observed and from which one can draw conclusions. With such a small and narrow data base, it is as if we were limited in our understanding of evolution to Darwin's observations of the turtles on the Galapagos Islands.

I mentioned earlier that the tradition in rumor research has been to concentrate on the three *C*'s. Not only do conflict, crisis, and catastrophe provide settings for rumors, but people are especially motivated to study them because they threaten the well-being of the society. World War II, for example, stimulated interest in rumors concerning the war effort and tensions between segments of the domestic population.

Broad generalizations have been made from the narrow observations of the three *C*'s studies. For instance, rumors have been causally related to breakdowns in official communication that occur in wars or disasters. Rumor study in World War II even presented something as scientifically impressive as a formula: Produced by Allport and Postman, it stated that "The two essential conditions of importance and ambiguity seem to be related to rumor transmission in a roughly quantitative manner. A formula for the intensity of rumor might be written as follows: $R \sim i \times a$."[10]

In words, this formula means that the amount of rumor in circulation will vary with the importance of the subject to the individuals concerned times the ambiguity of the evidence pertaining to the topic at issue. The relation between importance and ambiguity is not additive but multiplicative, for if either importance or ambiguity is zero, there is no rumor. Given the nature of crises, with matters of personal or national survival occupying people's minds (importance) in a context of confusion, censorship, or conspiracy (ambiguity), this formula and the points of view it represents seem appropriate in wartime. However, I am not sure that it is applicable to *all* rumor situations, any more than is the occurrence of media failure always applicable. All of which is to say that the limitations on these types of studies place a limit on the generalizations that can be derived.

Focus of the Book

I would like to add another *C* to those mentioned: It stands for *commerce*. Commercial rumors, in fact, will be the primary topic of this book—hearsay about products and producers such as the McDonald's or Procter & Gamble rumors. Such rumors have been around for a long time, but in the past several years they have loomed into prominence. These occurrences may be a function of the increasing number of national corporations that deal with consumers. A rumor about a locally owned grocery store would not attract nationwide attention from the public or from social psychologists. However, there are fewer and fewer locally owned retail stores, and those that do exist sell products that are produced by national organizations. Similarly, there are fewer local restaurants and more franchises; fewer local breweries, bottling companies, bakeries, and so forth. Thus, a rumor about a product or producer today is likely to be of wide geographic interest.

In addition, media—especially television—have become very important in people's lives, and advertising has made products and producers familiar to the population in a manner unknown in previous decades. Most people are familiar with and interested in the top companies. A rumor about such a company is likely to go coast to coast because the target is a big, coast-to-coast outfit. As a consequence, public information officers are much more concerned about rumors than they used to be. As one professor of business administration told me, "The thought of rumor strikes dread into the hearts of corporate officials." Indeed, people tend to fear things they do not understand. This book can allay the fear of rumor by promoting understanding. Although my specific concern is with commercial rumors, these will necessarily be examined in the general context of previous research on rumors in general.

Darwin's insights about evolution had to be tested and expanded beyond his observations of the turtles on the Galapagos Islands. Similarly, much of what has been thought about rumors must be examined further because of the limitations of the current three *C*'s data base. I hope to apply what is generally known about rumors to rumors in the marketplace. I also hope that what I have learned in the marketplace can, in turn, be a contribution to the general theory of rumors.

Outline of the Chapters

Chapter 2 consists of a case study of the McDonald's Corporation experience with rumor. It is a particularly good example because it involves both types of commercial rumor and just about everything else we will be discussing in this book.

Chapter 3 begins the analysis of commercial rumors by identifying the basic components involved and examines reasons why people participate in the rumor process.

Chapter 4 deals with the content of the stories. Questions addressed include: Where do they come from? How do they start? Conspiracy rumors also are taken up in this section.

Chapter 5 discusses contamination rumors. Similarities to and differences from conspiracy rumors are examined.

Chapter 6 is devoted to the process by which rumors are transmitted. Several models described in the rumor literature are examined to see how well they apply to commercial rumors.

Chapter 7 deals with the various ways mass media play a part in rumor.

Chapter 8 reports on some research stimulated by commercial rumors.

Chapter 9 looks at rumor in the stock market.

Chapter 10 draws on what has preceded and outlines some applied rumor psychology specifically aimed at preventing and/or extinguishing a rumor.

In sum, rumors traditionally have been studied in the context of conflict, crisis, and catastrophe. The focus of this book is on commercial rumors, those types dealing with products and producers. Case studies are presented, and discussion includes motivations for telling rumors, how conspiracy and contamination rumors come about, the structure of communications networks, and applications of rumor control.

Endnotes

1. People ask, "What is the Church of Satan?" Early in Christian history, Gnostic movements and other groups influenced by Persian dualism believed that there were opposing powers, and that one could choose to follow Satan as an alternative to following Christ. In the Middle Ages the Church accused witches of being in league with the Devil in order to obtain supernatural powers, and even today Christians tend to lump witchcraft and Satanism together. Contemporary witches deny this link-up. Marcello Truzzi, a sociologist at Eastern Michigan University, says that they claim to be practicing a type of "folk-magic" that predates Christianity. He identifies four types of Satanic groups currently existing in the United States. One is the Gnostic tradition, in which the followers have a non-heretical belief in a devil who is an angel to be worshipped. The second type includes "sex clubs" that use satanic trappings; many of these are sadomasochistic flagellation societies. Another variety is the drug and acid groups that sort of make up their Satanism as they go along. The Charles Manson bunch is the best known of this ilk.

   The most prominent movement, however, is the Church of Satan in San Francisco, headed by the High Priest Anton Szandor Lavey. Founded in 1965 on Walpurgisnacht (the eve of May Day, a witches' sabbath), it is estimated to have about 7000 members. There are three "Grottos" in the Bay Area and some more scattered around the country. Truzzi describes their tenets as follows in "The Occult Revival as Popular Culture: Some Random Observations on the Old and Nouveau Witch," an article in *The Sociological Quarterly*, Volume 13, No. 1 (1972):

   > *In its major features, the Church of Satan takes the position of extreme Machiavellianism and cynical-realism toward the nature of man. It has many philosophical parallels with philosophies as divergent in sophistication as the Superman views of Friedrich Nietzche and the Objectivist ideals of Ayn Rand. Its major feature, however, is its emphasis upon the importance of myth and magic and upon their impact in a world of people who can still be manipulated through such beliefs and emotions. This Satanist, then, is the ultimate pragmatist.*
   >
   > *The predominant form of Satanism does not represent a new mysticism at all. It not only denies the existence of anything supernatural or spiritual but it even condemns any narcotics, hallucinogens, or other agents that might act to separate rational man from his material environment. This Satanist does not seek escape from reality: he wishes full control of reality and is even willing to use all forces—including irrational elements—that help him in achieving his desired ends.*

2. Webster, Noah, *Webster's New International Dictionary of the English Language* (Springfield, Mass.: G & C Merriam Company, 1952).

3. Rosnow, Ralph, and Gary Fine, *Rumor and Gossip* (New York: Elsevier, 1976).
4. Virgil, *Aeneid IV* (New York: Harper & Brothers Publishers, 1855), p. 72. (Translation provided by Professor Joseph Poe, Classics Department, Tulane University).
5. Shibutani, Tomatso, *Improvised News* (Indianapolis: Bobbs-Merrill, 1966).
6. Rosnow and Fine, *op. cit.*
7. Knopf, Terry, *Rumors, Race and Riots* (New Brunswick, N.J.: Transaction Books, 1975).
8. Odum, Howard W., *Race and Rumors of Race* (Chapel Hill: University of North Carolina Press, 1943).
9. Allport, Gordon, and Leo J. Postman, *The Psychology of Rumor* (New York: Henry Holt, 1947).
10. Allport and Postman, *op. cit.*, pp. 33, 34.

Chapter Two

THE CASE OF McDONALD'S CORPORATION: A RUMORED LINK TO THE CHURCH OF SATAN

On Thursday, August 25, 1977, the Corporate Communications Division of McDonald's Corporation of Oakbrook, Illinois, received three letters in the 2 P.M. mail. A letter from Piqua, Ohio asked about the sizeable donations made by Ray Kroc, the President of McDonald's, to the Church of Satan. Two more letters from the same geographic area asked similar questions. Doug Timberlake, head of Corporate Communications, was surprised and puzzled.[1] McDonald's subsequently wrote back, denying the allegation against Kroc and adding reassurance of its good reputation. Strange as the letters were, the public relations people thought little about them.[2] They had no inkling that they were on the verge of an experience with mass behavior which would persist for the next three years.

Of course, the rumor did not start on August 25th. Nobody knows how long it had been circulating before it came to the attention of McDonald's, although usually someone calls or writes to verify a particular rumor shortly after it begins. The Piqua letter was somewhat atypical in that it assumed the truth of the story; the writer just wanted to clarify the details concerning the mechanics of Kroc's Satan connection. Usually, companies hear from "friends" of the product who want to be told that the rumor is not true.

9

Similar letters continued to come in, a few at a time. By Christmas of 1977 a total of 13 inquiries had been received. When the public relations people began keeping track of the postmarks on a map, most of the pins were in the Ohio and Indiana area. By January the situation was getting out of hand. The tracking map now showed the rumor spreading out of the Ohio Valley pocket, and letters began to come from other parts of the country.

When the rumor hit Texas, Arkansas, and Oklahoma, Doug Timberlake likened it to an explosion.[3] Letters and phone calls came in from clergymen, patrons, and McDonald's owner-operators, all referring to the story that Ray Kroc gave 35 percent of his earnings to the Church of Satan. The people asking about the rumor almost always knew a co-worker who had a daughter, or a friend who had a mother-in-law, or a pastor who had a parishioner who had "actually" seen Ray Kroc make the declaration on the *Johnny Carson Show, 60 Minutes, 20/20, Phil Donahue, Merv Griffin, Tom Snyder,* or the *Today Show.*

Fighting the Fire Locally

The strategy at Oakbrook was to douse each fire locally as it flared up.[4] A standard letter was composed to respond to general inquiries. A suggested form letter was sent to management, and Ray Kroc prepared a letter for clergymen. In addition, specially devised "extinguishers" could be called upon, such as letters of support from prominent clergymen deploring the rumors and attesting to Mr. Kroc's Christian integrity as well as to McDonald's multi-faceted community contributions. There were letters from the producers of *60 Minutes,* and *20/20* stating that Ray Kroc had never been on their programs. He *had* appeared on *Phil Donahue, Merv Griffin, Tom Snyder,* and the *Today Show* during 1977, but these appearances were in connection with promotion of his recently published auto-biography, *Grinding It Out.*[5] They also made available official verbatim transcripts, with cover letters from the producers, to demonstrate that nothing was said about the Church of Satan on any of the programs.[6] The campaign was active and effective, but as soon as one area of the country was controlled, there would be a flare-up somewhere else. On several occasions

Timberlake himself met with ministerial groups, bringing the written affidavits, the transcripts, and sometimes tapes of the programs.[7] These meetings did not occur very often, but several times a group of owner-operators who feared a militant organized boycott in an area asked for help. On one of these occasions in Oklahoma, the ministers and McDonald's managers assembled in a conference room where one of the ministers arose and declared that on a previous Wednesday, at a meeting of the men's club of his church, one of his parishioners had announced that he himself had seen Ray Kroc make that statement on television. Timberlake responded, "This may be the man we are looking for." After the meeting he asked if he could have the man's name. The next day Timberlake went to the man's auto-repair shop and told him that he was checking out a story about the head of McDonald's being on a television program. When the man was asked if he had seen the event on television, he vigorously denied it. Such a response usually ends any attempt to track a rumor, for it means starting the search all over again.[8]

Rekindling the Blaze

The campaign chugged along. Inquiries came in steadily by phone and mail, and just as steadily the denials and explanations were sent out. Almost a year after it all began, things appeared to be cooling down, and the volume of mail decreased ever so slightly. Then, on July 2, 1978, a former parishioner of the Dayton, Ohio Kenmore Church of God returned from Chicago and visited her former pastor at his church. As she chatted with him, she made a point of passing on the McDonald's rumor. She confirmed the reverend's suspicion about the dire straits the world was in by telling him that Ray Kroc, the head of McDonald's, was giving 35 percent of his profits to the Church of Satan. So that he would have no doubts about the matter, she stated that she herself saw Ray Kroc making that statement on the *Phil Donahue Show.*[9]

One would hope that a religious leader, upon hearing that kind of sensational news, would contact someone at the McDonald's Corporation to confirm its truth. But that was just what the reverend did *not* do. (Surprisingly, few clergymen who heard the rumor bothered to check it out before passing it on.)

He simply accepted the story as "gospel truth" and promptly published it in his church newsletter.

This newsletter not only went out to his parishioners but also was picked up by other pastors looking for items for *their* newsletters.[10] In addition, he himself littered the country with 200 more "special" newsletters to former congregation members, clergymen, friends, and other interested parties.[11]

It is easy to see how the Kroc-Satan story fanned out across the country. The rumor became a conflagration, especially in the mid-southern and southeastern United States. Organized boycotts against McDonald's were called for by anti-Satan contingents.[12] Franchise operators began phoning to ask what McDonald's was going to do to help them. Timberlake's standard approach remained to put out the fire where it occurred. The first place was the Dayton Kenmore Church of God. The original newsletter did not show up at McDonald's offices, but reprints of it from other church newsletters surfaced. The reverend was contacted and given all the standard rebuttal material; he was also strongly encouraged to issue a retraction, which he did.[13]

A Stubborn Case

Threats of organized boycotts caused owner-operators to ask Timberlake to meet with groups of clergy in Alabama and Florida. During a meeting in the latter state, the McDonald's people had the most bizarre confrontation of the whole experience. They met with a pastor and a young parishioner who claimed that she herself had seen the *Phil Donahue Show* in which Ray Kroc said that he contributed 35 percent of his profits to the Church of Satan. Based on her report, the pastor had called for a boycott of McDonald's. When confronted, she did not demur as the others had done. She did not deny that she had said such a thing or claim that she heard it from her sister-in-law or a truck driver; rather she *herself* had seen the program in question and had reported it to her pastor! The stage was set for the showing of a videotape of the *Phil Donahue Show* provided by an affiliate station in the area. (The tape, of course, was untouched by anyone from McDonald's.) When the tape was run through the viewer, not even the slightest hint of anything to do with the Church of Satan appeared. Was the matter now settled for the young lady and her pastor? Not at all. She remained adamant, and the minister produced a set of notes, written by her on long sheets of lined yellow paper, which included a verbatim copy of the script both leading up to the alleged Kroc-Satan declaration and following it. How she was able to reproduce such an accurate copy of the script is a puzzling question; she may have a photographic memory, or she may have seen the written transcript of the show which had been in the minister's possession for some time. She offered no explanation for the discrepancies between what she said and what was presented on the tape. The pastor may or may not have been convinced, but it was obvious that hard evidence was on McDonald's side and that further agitation such as a boycott would be unwise.[14]

The Story Goes "National"

At about this time, a Florida-based "action-line" reporter called McDonald's to make some inquiries about the Satan rumor. She became interested in the topic of the Satan rumor itself and called back to ask how long it had been going on, how widespread it was, and how much paper, labor, and money had been used to battle the rumor. She thought this story interesting, so she wrote it up as an item for the Knight-Ridder News Service. Timberlake and associates had responded to many action-line reporters concerning the false allegations of the rumors, but until now they had chosen not to go public on the matter. The Knight-Ridder story made the matter public.

The *Chicago Sun-Times* called about the rumor and wrote it up for their news syndicate. The wire services picked it up, and it went all over the country. At this point, Timberlake put on the lid: no more interviews, no more public statements. He decided to deal with the problem locally, as he had in the past. The campaign continued, and how long it would have gone on is anybody's guess. Some people had a premonition that the rumor was showing signs of burning out. We will never know for sure, however, because the Satan rumor was ended by a most effective but undesirable event—the appearance of another, more damaging rumor.

A Whole New Can of Worms

Toward the end of the summer of 1978 I told my mother-in-law
what I had learned concerning the ongoing episode of the Kroc-
Satan rumors. She said that she, too, found rumors interesting
and that, in fact, she had heard a new rumor about a hamburger chain: A story going around Chattanooga, Tennessee,
alleged that Wendy's put red worms in their hamburgers! She
did not know how widespread the rumor was, but she had
heard it more than once.

Contamination rumors are fairly common occurrences in the
food and beverage industries. They often sound silly and seem
merely bothersome, but they can be devastating, as Wendy's
well knew. The first inquiring phone call was made to Wendy's
on August 15th. The caller said that the worm story had
appeared on the television program *20/20*. As the calls poured
in, however, the name of the television program involved
changed from week to week. Sometimes it was *20/20*, sometimes *60 Minutes*.

Very early in this rumor series, a woman called Wendy's
main office to say that her husband saw a program (*20/20*) on
which appeared representatives from Wendy's and Mc-
Donald's hamburger chains. The Wendy's people, she said,
admitted to putting worms in their hamburgers, but the
McDonald's spokesmen were noncommittal. Wendy's was the
main target of the worm rumor, with McDonald's, Burger Chef,
and Burger King named from time to time. Steve Samons of
Wendy's conferred with Doug Timberlake of McDonald's
several times. There was some concern at McDonald's about
the possible spreading of the Wendy's rumor, but McDonald's
was still expending most of its energies on the Satan problem.
During the first week of September, however, McDonald's
heard from the Chattanooga Better Business Bureau that inquiries were being made about worms in its meat. Managers
also began to get calls about the worm situation, but still the
McDonald's problem did not compare to Wendy's.

After Labor Day the Wendy's worm rumors became even
stronger in the Chattanooga area and included adjoining parts
of Georgia. One whole section of Atlanta was affected. In
desperation, Wendy's Chattanooga people demanded that the
head office do something. Samons decided to go public, while
Timberlake opted to "lie in the weeds" and see how Wendy's

made out. A television news conference was scheduled for September 15th. It was to feature a representative of the government meat inspection office in that region who would point out that nothing was added to the ground beef at Wendy's or at any other fast-food chain. For some reason, he did not show up, so the production became exclusively Wendy's, who denied all and made statements to exonerate themselves. After that effort, they were never again part of the rumor scene.[15]

The Worm Turns—On McDonald's

From then on the rumor involved McDonald's. It spread out from Chattanooga and for a while seemed to follow Interstate 75, over to Atlanta, up to Ohio. Doug Timberlake said that when it reached Indiana and Ohio, it really flared up.

McDonald's response was much the same as their response to the Satan rumor: They dealt with it locally, denying it immediately, getting names and sending out letters, and passing out literature. It just so happened that McDonald's had an illustrated promotion press kit, featuring the high quality of ingredients that went into their burgers—"Nothing but 100% pure United States Government-inspected ground beef," and so forth. These materials were distributed to franchise owners in the affected areas and guidelines were laid down. If the literature did not seem to quell the rumors, it was recommended that they start a small, local advertising campaign stressing quality of products, with no specific mention of the rumor. If that failed to work, they were told to go to the local press as a last resort. In no case, however, were they to use the worm *worm*. Managers who called to ask questions about the rumor problem elsewhere were told what to do "just in case."

Then things turned scorching hot in Ohio, Tennessee, and Georgia. This genre of rumor did not allow for the deliberate procedures used in the Satan campaign. Upon hearing the previous rumor, some people were upset by the purported Satan connection, many did not care at all, and a few might have been attracted by the "campy" suggestion; *nobody*, however, liked the idea of worms in their hamburger meat. UGH! It wasn't even necessary for a person to find the rumor credible in order for it to affect his behavior. Just the thought in the back of one's mind of worms in hamburgers was enough to steer one to a pizza parlor. As Doug Timberlake said, "The rumor was hitting at the bottom line. It was seriously affecting sales in certain areas, and these kinds of losses could not be sustained for a very long period. The afflicted franchises were hurting; their operations were getting badly mauled."[16]

Time for Decision

The ongoing marketing survey carried out by McDonald's tacked on a rumor question in order to survey the extent of the damage. Those surveyed were asked on the telephone, "Have you heard rumors about any fast-food operation?" The heaviest concentrations of rumors were found in Cincinnati and Atlanta, where 75 percent of the people surveyed said they had heard the rumor. In Atlanta, in particular, a large portion of the respondents had heard the rumor and many believed it. The rumor problem had assumed what Timberlake called a "critical mass," and it had to be confronted with force immediately. Time was becoming very short.[17]

It was decided to hold a press conference in Atlanta. Timberlake was aware that "going public" would make many people aware of the rumor who had never heard it before. Public relations people often are leery of talking directly about a rumor problem or referring to rumors even indirectly, because they believe that such tactics spread rumor even more. On the other hand, an emphatic public statement possibly could immunize people from the effects of the rumor when they did hear it, as well as set the record straight for those who had already heard it. On November 23rd a national press conference was held in Atlanta in which the rumor about "protein additives" was denied. The "100 % U.S. Government-inspected beef" position was re-asserted, and of course the word "worm" was never mentioned.[18] A follow-up nationwide advertising campaign was launched in which color photographs of the product, with captions, celebrated its pure, uncontaminated ingredients.[19] The "extinguishers" went into effect, and shortly thereafter the rumor was quenched.

With fire-fighting, rumor-fighting, or any activity in which there is a crowd of onlookers, one finds a lot of second-guessers. Some people connected with McDonald's said that they should have gone public sooner, should have waited longer, or should not have gone public at all. The fire was out, but the atmosphere in Oakbrook, Illinois, had a fallout of acrimonious ash.[20]

Endnotes

1. Carter, Malcolm, "False Rumor Puts Bite on Big Mac," Associated Press, *New Orleans Times-Picayune* (November 19, 1978).
2. Feyder, Susan, "Rumor of Gift to Satan Cult Plays Devil with McDonald's," *Chicago Tribune* (October 10, 1978).
3. Timberlake, Doug, personal conversation (December 12, 1980).
4. Feyder, Susan, *op. cit.*
5. Timberlake, Doug, *op. cit.*
6. Carter, Malcolm, *op. cit.*
7. Associated Press, "Profits Not Going to Hell, Chain Says," *New Orleans Times-Picayune* (October 11, 1978).
8. Timberlake, Doug, *op. cit.*
9. Knight-Ridder News Service, "Satan Rumor Bedevils McDonald's Founder," St. Paul *Pioneer Press* (October 8, 1978).
10. Carter, Malcolm, *op. cit.*
11. Timberlake, Doug, *op. cit.*
12. Feyder, Susan, *op. cit.*
13. Knight-Ridder News Service, *op. cit.*
14. Timberlake, Doug, *op. cit.*
15. Timberlake, Doug, *op. cit.*
16. Timberlake, Doug, *op. cit.*
17. Timberlake, Doug, *op. cit.*
18. Reetz, John, "McDonald's Denies Tale as Just a Can of Worms," *Atlanta Journal* (November 15, 1978).
19. Goggins, Susan, M., *The Wormburger Scare: A Case Study of The McDonald's Corporation Public Relation Campaign to Stop a Damaging Rumor.* Master's Thesis, Georgia State University, Athens, Georgia (1979).
20. Greene, Bob, "Trying to Unravel a Can of Worms," *Washington Star* (November 24, 1978).

Chapter Three

THE WHO AND
THE WHY OF RUMORS

If we want to understand why commercial rumors are circulated and who tells them, it may be advisable to examine the structure and function of rumors. Essentially a rumor involves passing along a brief message including bits of information. This form of communication is in contrast to legend which, although very similar to rumor in many ways, tends to be a developed story—usually with a surprise ending. If one is interested in these tales, Jan Brunvand writes about what he calls "urban lore" in the book *The Vanishing Hitchhiker.*[1] In commercial rumors the bits of information can be categorized into three components: ·

1. *The Target.* Commercial enterprises and the products, policies, and personalities associated with them can be the target of rumors—for example, Ray Kroc of McDonald's in the Satanism rumor, and McDonald's product, hamburgers, in the worm rumor.

2. *The Charge or Allegation.* The rumor makes a *point* about the target. In the McDonald's example, one rumor charged collusion with the Church of Satan and the other claimed that worms were used in hamburgers. These examples represent the two basic types of allegation found in commercial rumors: *conspiracy* and *contamination,* respectively. Conspiracy rumors tell of policies or practices promoted by a commercial enterprise that are deemed threatening or ideologically undesirable to the people participating in the rumor. Contamination rumors

claim that a certain feature of a commercial product is
harmful or undesirable.

3. *The Source.* The message is often attributed to an
    authoritative source to give it credibility. The reference
    may be direct or indirect, specific or vague. In the Mc-
    Donald's case there were variations such as, "I heard it
    on the *Phil Donahue Show*" or "My sister-in-law told
    me."

The "component" concept of the rumor message is validated
by the fact that the three parts are often interchanged in
various rumors. An allegation can be associated with different
targets, and a target can have several allegations circulating.
Also, different sources can be identified with the above. The
combinations are similar to a Tinker Toy Construction Set in
which several structures can be built from the same parts.

I have coined terms for the two processes involving the
combinations just described. When a single allegation hits two
different targets it is called a "divergent rumor process." An
example is when both Wendy's and McDonald's were hit by
the worm rumor. A single target being hit by two allegations
exemplifies a "convergent rumor process." This process
occurred when McDonald's was hit by both the Satan rumor
and the worm rumor.

The Transmitting Population

Rumor analysis also requires consideration of the participants.
Each has a dual function in that one listens to the message and
in turn passes it on. If the rumor is not passed on, it is "dead-
ended," and whether or not this event occurs depends on the
nature of the population. The situation is analagous to a spark
landing on a cement sidewalk and burning out because there is
no flammable reception, as there would be if the spark landed
on dry grass. A primary requirement for rumor survival is that
the message be relevant to the people involved. Items about
interest rates will have wider circulation on Wall Street than
they will in a junior high school. Commercial rumors vary as to
how specific or general their relevance must be to the carrying
population. In the case of conspiracy rumors, it usually is a
select group that regards the messages as relevant. In the case

cited in the previous chapter it was found that the rumor about the Church of Satan ran through groups of Christian fundamentalists who care about Satan and his sinister maneuverings. Segments of the population who do not believe that Satan exists or care about his followers' financial arrangements will not be likely to hear or to pass on the message.

Contamination rumors, on the other hand, tend to circulate in a more general population, but even here some relevance is important. It is safe to assume that no one wants red worms in one's ground meat and that therefore the story will be of interest to everyone. A study done at Northwestern University,[2] however, showed that among students who had been presented with information concerning worms as an acceptable form of food there was less impact from the message than there was among a group who had not been exposed to the possibility of worms as food. The obvious explanation is that if one does not mind the thought of eating worms, the story loses relevance. In another example, Frenchmen would not likely be upset about allegations of horsemeat being in hamburgers, whereas most Americans would be, because horsemeat is commonly eaten in France but not in the United States. Contamination rumors may also have special populations delimited by the users of the product. For instance, children are the main consumers of bubble gum and certain types of candy, and they therefore are the population passing on rumors concerning those products.

Allport and Postman refer to these populations as "rumor publics," and they make the following observations:[3]

> *Each rumor has its own public. Financial rumors circulate principally among those whose fortunes can be affected by the ups and downs of the market. Rumors about changes in the draft law, in income tax rates, or about projected housing developments will spread mostly among those who are potentially affected. Children in school, all eager for a holiday, will seize greedily upon reports of a pending "teachers' meeting" or of necessary repairs on the school building. Occupational and social groups all have their peculiar susceptibilities. Physicians, clergymen, aviators, or stag parties will launch into tales that reflect the common interest of the groups. A rumor public exists wherever there is a community of interest.*

In review, rumors are made up of components of a message including an allegation, a target, and a source, and they are carried by a population that considers the message relevant.

But what makes people listen to and pass on hearsay? What is required are explanations for why some people participate in rumors and some do not and identification of the particular rewards for those who do. As we examine the various reasons individually, it is well to keep in mind that, with actual situations and people, any given reason is not self-contained and mutually exclusive, and that there may be several factors operating simultaneously.

Rumors as Diversion

If a message is to survive as a rumor, it must be interesting. In Allport and Postman's formula $R \sim i \times a$, the i stands for importance.[4] In the "three C's" situations most of the items were important in that they related to tense and threatening circumstances. Lately, the generality and significance of "importance" have been questioned.[5] Perhaps importance is too limited a term. The essential feature is that the message is attention-getting or interesting—and that which is interesting is not always important. The principle operating here is a version of one of W.I. Thomas's[6] four basic wishes: the wish for new experience. This wish implies that each person has an exploratory drive that makes him seek out and be receptive to unique, titillating events which jazz up life. Rumors that touch on the unusual, grotesque, or surprising will do just that. They may or may not be important, but they are interesting and attention-getting.

People do not engage in activities very long unless they are positively reinforced at some level of their experience. This fact has puzzled many social scientists when it comes to rumors, because rumors are often repulsive, frightening, discouraging, or negative in their content. Obviously, then, the nature of the content does not necessarily make a rumor experience an un-rewarding one. We have had frequent observations about the amount of "bad news" in the daily papers. The fact that everything is going all right and normal is by definition a non-unique, non-noteworthy event. Bad news, however, is different and attention-getting. For the same reason, negative messages in rumors make them compelling. Information about misfortune or negative events is a different, "non-normal," intriguing deviation from the routine.

Rosnow and Fine,[7] in their discussion of the widespread false reports of the death of one of the Beatles in the late sixties, point out that "an important attribute of the McCartney rumor... is its amusement and entertainment value." Stories about the Church of Satan or worms in hamburgers also are certainly attention-getters.

It must also be pointed out that the level of interest provided by a theme is relative to the context. In circumstances heavy with boredom, bits of "news" or gossip are seized upon with alacrity, and passed on through a network of people until something evolves that is interesting, lively, and able to relieve drabness. Anyone who has served time in the military knows that rumor can be a dominant pastime. There are several reasons for this circumstance, but one in particular is a state of inactivity, waiting, or tedium and a general lack of anything to fill a cognitive void. In such circumstances, the "interest" factor is relative to what else is going on and it may not take much to make an item interesting. A rumor can be only mildly interesting and still be picked up because of the unstimulating atmosphere.

In all these instances, rumor and gossip serve the same function—that of titillation and breaking monotony. An example of such a commercial rumor is the low-intensity but persistent complaint that Tab contains 86 calories (instead of the one calorie as advertised). This information may be relevant to weight-conscious soft-drink consumers, but it is certainly not high on the general scale of importance. Over the past couple of years I have asked my students about it, and it seems fairly widespread. I also asked them under what circumstance they heard the charge made; it is usually a form of small talk in the course of a dull, uneventful phase of a social event such as a double date.

Rumor as News

Another feature that frequently accompanies the "humdrum" scene is a lack of any *bona fide* information about what is going on concerning a situation. Again using the military as an example, they not only have long periods of collective inaction but there is also an absence of any news about what is happening and what the next move will be. The combination of lack of information and a strong interest in what is going on makes one very receptive to any communication—and unverified bits are better than none at all. Accordingly, some very outlandish tales circulate. In the Army, under circumstances described above, I remember stories going around about our company being shipped to Poland, bulldozer school, or Antarctica. Corporation bureaucracies also often have limited flows of official information, and the office grapevine is a natural expression for the need to talk about job promotions and other matters related to one's life.

This model of lack of information and subsequent filling of a vacuum is a basic one for Tomatso Shibutani.[8] The orientation is reflected in the title of his book, *Improvised News.* As we have mentioned before, hearsay may be valued because certain groups do not have access to the news as a result of their position in the organizational structure. There are other situations in which news is absent because there is an actual breakdown in the media capacities. These occurrences are usually related to the three *C*'s where natural disasters, bombings, or riots have physically disrupted communication channels.

The information problem in the above is different from the one which results from direct policy. During wartime there is censorship and withholding of news for security, morale, and other reasons. That practice is one of the reasons that rumors are so plentiful during wartime. Attendant to the suppression and control of the news is a "subjective lack of news," because people do not trust the news they do get. In totalitarian countries, hearsay becomes a very important part of everyday life.[9]

The Need for Meaning and Structure

Turmoil, upheaval, and disruptions of various kinds bring about not only an absence of news but also a heightened desire to receive some information on the part of the people affected because of the disruption of the status quo.

While humans are attracted to the new, the unusual, and the innovative, most of us "don't want too much, thank you," because we also have a strong need for security. We look for completion, structure, what the Gestalt theorists in psychology call "closure." We cannot exist for long in the midst of vagueness or uncertainty. For instance, we avoid being in the dark and we find uncharted futures ominous. We don't like to think about death unless our culture provides a scenario of what to expect. Catastrophes such as floods, earthquakes, and hurricanes not only result in physical breakdowns in normal communication networks but also increase the need for structure by shattering normal patterns and expectations because of the crisis. During such chaotic times a population will seek out or create information by way of rumors in their search for structure. People will eagerly look for messages that give meaning to what is happening. In Prasad's[10] account of an earthquake in India, he tells how, in the aftermath, word was passed on that this calamity was "just" part of a worldwide series of earthquakes that would destroy the world. Bad as the "news" was, the rumored version gave some explanation for what was occurring and was picked up and transmitted by the population because structure and meaning had been brought to the chaotic scene.

Smelser[11] says that rumors about Nazi or Ku Klux Klan instigations of the Detroit race riots were an attempt to explain what was an non-understandable event to many of that city's population. Shibutani tells how people in California explained the success of the Pearl Harbor attack by spreading rumors about local Japanese treachery:[12]

The attack had obviously been well planned. How had the enemy been able to plan so carefully, catching the entire area off guard? Where had he gotten the detailed information necessary to execute it with such precision? The finger pointed directly at Hawaii's 160,000 residents of Japanese ancestry, and hundreds of rumors arose implicating them. Among the most widespread of these rumors were: a McKinley High School ring was found on the body of a Japanese flier shot down over Honolulu; the water supply had been poisoned by the local Japanese; Japanese plantation workers had cut arrows pointing to Pearl Harbor in the canefields of Oahu; the local Japanese had been notified of the time of attack by an advertisement in a Honolulu newspaper on December 6; Nisei armed with machine guns drove up to the main gate at Pearl Harbor in trucks and, as the side panels dropped off, shot down marines; automobiles driven by local Japanese blocked the roads from Honolulu to Pearl Harbor; Japanese residents waved their kimonos at the pilots and signaled to them; some local men were dressed in Japanese Army uniforms during the attack.

What we are talking about is related to the *a* portion of the Allport and Postman formula $R \sim i \times a$, which stands for ambiguity. In the above examples the lack of clarity comes from the absence of news and/or from confusing situations because of chaotic events.

An experiment involving a similar phenomenon was conducted by Schacter and Burdick[13] in which an ambiguous event or one of "cognitive unclarity" was contrived at a girls' preparatory school:[14]

> *On the day of the study, between 8:25 and 8:35, the principal of the school went into four different classrooms. In each class, she interrupted the work, stood in front of the class, pointed a finger at one girl, and announced, "Miss K., would you get your hat, coat, and books, please, and come with me. You will be gone for the rest of the day." Then, without a word, she and the girl walked out of the room together. Such an action was completely unprecedented in the experience of the girls. To insure that the event remained a complete mystery, the entire staff of the school had been instructed to reply to any questions about the event that "they knew nothing about it."*

In addition to the cognitively unclear event that was staged, a "rumor" was systematically planted in some of the classes:[15]

> *A day or two before the study took place, various teachers made appointments for 8:15 on the morning of the study to see each of the eight girls with whom the rumor was to be planted. Ostensibly, the purpose of these appointments was to discuss academic progress, next year's program, and other such matters. This was routine procedure. Each of these interviews followed an identical pattern. After six or seven minutes of discussing the matter for which the appointment had presumably been arranged, and immediately before terminating the interview, each teacher said, "By the way, some examinations have been taken from the office. Do you happen to know anything about this?" No such thing had taken place and, of course, all of the girls interviewed denied any knowledge of the affair. The interview was so timed that each of the girls returned to her classroom before the principal entered any of the rooms.*

The conditions were distributed over the three classes. One class had eight of its students exposed to a rumor stimulus when the principal asked them about the stolen exams. Another class was presented with an ambiguous occurrence by having one of its members called out of the room without any explanation. In the third class, eight of its members were presented with the rumor stimuli about the exams and then allowed to return to class, but no one was yet called out of the class. The same class then experienced the ambiguous event when a girl was summoned out of the room. The investigators later asked the students of the three classes if they had heard any rumors. The classes that had the planted rumor exposure *and* the ambiguous event exhibited more rumor activity than the classes with the other two conditions. The conclusion was that the rumor helped explain the ambiguous dismissal of the student.

Commercial Rumors as News and Meaning

Although the "failure of the media" approach was derived from other types of data, it can often be applied to the rumors we are focusing on in this book. The conspiracy type of rumor, by definition, implies that some things going on are being hidden from the public. People who are amenable to a conspiracy theory are less likely to trust establishment news sources to tell "the full story." Their suspicious bent would make them chary and receptive to alternative information.

Conditions such as catastrophe, conflict, or suppression may seem to be far removed from anything dealing with rumors in the marketplace. Nevertheless, similar responses are involved in commercial rumors, although the precipitating events may not appear as dramatic. In like manner, commercial rumors can provide structure in a world where things seem jumbled and can help explain what is happening.

The need for structure comes about for different reasons with different groups. That is why certain rumors are rife in a specific population, and that is why attempts at understanding a rumor need to focus upon the particular people involved as well as on the rumor content.

Most people who see segments of their life turned upside down look for answers that give meaning and structure in terms of their subjective world or *schema*. It may not be an earthquake or a riot, but a group can have their own particular version of chaos and look for an appropriate accounting for it.

Followers of conservative religious persuasions in a rapidly changing social order can find much that is disturbing: Celebrities having children without being married. A "First Lady" saying that premarital sex may not be all that wrong. Gays flagrantly coming out of the closet and demanding their rights. Sex, nudity, and wanton indulgence the dominant themes in television, recordings, and films. Professional athletes being exposed as drug traffickers and addicts. All in all, what is happening to our nation? *It is going to the devil!*

If you believe that Satan is an active force and has dedicated followers, then Satanism-witchcraft rumors may just make sense out of all that is going on. In fact, for many fundamentalist religious groups, the rumor about Satan and his followers helps explain what is happening better than anything else. Also, conspiracy rumors are popular when they involve bizarre cults or secret organizations in that they leave one free to attribute all kinds of goings-on without much fear of contradiction because of the supposed hidden nature of their undertakings.

Rumor as Verification

As mentioned earlier, the content of the message may be relevant to only certain populations. The people involved have some need that matches up with the rumor. Hostile rumors about disliked groups usually serve a function for the rumor-bearer. For example, anti-black or anti-Semetic tales reinforce and justify one's feelings if one is hostile to those groups. In like manner a conspiracy involving the growing power of the Church of Satan can reconfirm one's cosmology and legitimate one's concern about the plot.

The rumor can do something else socially, in that the participating and sharing of the rumor can be rewarding as an interpersonal experience. Mrs. Pious wants to believe that there is a nudist conspiracy, and so she passes the rumor along to Mr. Grunch, who also wants to believe that there is a nudist conspiracy. In this process, they not only confirm their shared social reality but also strengthen their interpersonal relationship. The mutual head-nodding and eye-rolling in a rumor exchange is heavy reinforcement for people committed to a shared and related belief system.

Circle the Wagon—Us Against Them

The threat posed by a conspiracy can have a positive effect on a group as a whole. Can you imagine what it means to the morale of a fundamentalist religious group to have a real, live Satanic movement to rally against?

It is a common observation that nothing tends to unite a group more effectively than threats from an outside force. Social psychologists traditionally use the terms "in-group" and "out-group." In Sherif's[16] pioneering field experiment at a boys' camp, he arbitrarily selected members for two groups. They were given identifying names and were made to participate in competitive activities. At first the boys resented being separated from those in the other group. As competitive activities increased, however, the members felt an increase in cohesion and solidarity in their own group. Terry Knopf[17] writes that rumors "increase polarization while at the same time strengthening solidarity within each group—rumors create a common culture within which leadership mobilization and considered action can occur spontaneously."

Leaders try to take advantage of the competitiveness, conflict, or sense of threat that rumors can provide. When out-groups are socially distant, obscure, or secretive, one can fill in the information gap with hostile suppositions and not be contradicted. Also, if there is secrecy, normal news cannot be relied upon. Of course, if conspiracy rumors such as the Satanism stories are seized upon with eagerness by the faithful, think of what these rumors mean to the leaders of these religious groups. I don't mean the Billy Grahams, Jerry Falwells and Donald Wildmons; they do not need dubious conspiracies to bolster their positions of power. Rather, think of the lower echelon, the insecure shepherds with their unresponsive flocks. It is a very functional technique for a shaky minister to use conspiracy rumors to justify his bible-pounding admonitions of how evil the world has become. Every one provides further impetus to his calls for dedication and for heavier contributions.

An example of the function of alleged conspiracies is the one rumor concerning a petition filed by an atheist to force the Federal Communications Commission to abolish all religious broadcasting. Although such a petition has never been filed, this conspiracy rumor not only serves the purpose of promoting group cohesion and providing a rallying point but it also accomplishes it so well that the story has persisted for almost a decade. Wesley Jackson, a religious editor of the *New Orleans Times-Picayune* and *States-Item* writes:[18]

> *On repeated occasions, responsible religious publications, the secular press (Time, TV Guide, and others), and the FCSS have tried, to no avail, to advise the public that such a petition was never filed. But, repeatedly, certain religious factions, apparently with lots of idle money, start the rumor up again, using chain letters and good old-fashioned "scare tactics" that would have impressed Heinrich Himmler.*
>
> *To date, the FCC estimates, millions of dollars have been spent in postage alone, both by perpetrators of the rumor and by more than 13 million well-intentioned, but misguided and misled Americans who, in turn, have besieged the FCC, congressmen, and the media, and church leaders with mail protesting something that never was.*

Cutting Them Down to Size

In addition to the events threatening selected groups, there can be larger developments upsetting to the general population, such as inflation, recession, unemployment, international tensions, community conflicts, and the like. Many people throughout our society feel frustrated, threatened, and disturbed. Rumors sometimes can provide them with answers or explanations in a wider sense. Economic recessions, for example, are difficult to understand, and they can affect people from all levels of society, with lower strata usually the first and hardest hit. Members of fundamentalist religious groups are drawn largely from this section of society. Lately these people have had a double exposure to upsetting events: chaos in their own private worlds and chaos in the general economic sphere.

Middle class people also can lose their jobs, or be afraid they might lose them. Others become concerned about business being less than it should be. It is a common practice for people to engage in what is known as the comparison process, in which they gauge their own situation by looking at others. If others seem to be thriving and they are not, the comparison is an unpleasant one. Most people think of themselves as being virtuous and hardworking, and that used to be the only requirement for success—but no longer. How, then, can others be successful when we ourselves are not? How can one explain the success of McDonald's? A rumor may provide the answer.

Maybe they are really not above suspicion. Maybe they *are* connected with a nudist movement. Maybe they *do* put mammoth meat in their beef products. Maybe they *are* doing something else that is underhanded. Even if the rumor has minimal credibility as an explanation, it still can be a welcome thought. It reduces the size of the big guys, and makes for more acceptable comparisons. (How many middle-age women, for example, are gratified to hear that somewhere in this world tonight, Elizabeth Taylor is getting fat?)

Stress and Strain

One of the older and better known relationships in psychology is called the frustration-aggression hypothesis.[19] Over the years it has been modified, but the essential idea is that it is frustrating when things do not go well, and one can develop the urge to take it out on somebody else through aggression. An historic example was the relationship between the price of cotton and lynchings in the South: When the price went down, the number of lynchings went up.[20]

Generally it is thought that such aggression is directed against weaker targets, but the main point is that it is directed against targets that cannot fight back. Telling an unfavorable story about a corporation is certainly an act of hostility and, as officials of a target corporation will tell you, it is difficult to fight back. In any case, stressful times can bring about the frustration-aggression phenomenon, with hostile rumors being one of the possible aggressive responses. Stress also contributes to a person's anxiety, and anxiety is a major factor in rumor activity.

In two experiments, participants were tested with the Taylor Manifest Anxiety Scale before rumor simulation was started. Both studies showed that those subjects who were high in anxiety repeated the stories most frequently.[21, 22] Rumors are often an attempt to reduce ambiguity. Anxiety increases the need to reduce ambiguity. As Rosnow puts it:[23]

> By "anxiety" I mean a negative affective state that is produced by apprehension about an impending, potentially negative outcome. The cognitive factor can be called uncertainty or unpredictability, by which I mean a belief or intellectual state that is produced by doubt, as when events are unstable, capricious, or problematical.

These two conditions, when stimulated by ongoing events, seem to be linearly related to rumor strength. When there is little anxiety or uncertainty elicited by the situation, the low levels of arousal engender no rumors to dissipate the emotional and cognitive states. At the other extreme, the more stressful and unpredictable a situation is, the greater is the resulting discomfort and therefore the more urgent is the desire to reduce anxiety or uncertainty.

Experimental studies have shown that the need for certainty and the extremeness of response are both related to anxiety. The most influential and comprehensive study, however, was the series called the "Authoritarian Personality,"[24] designed to get at the "roots of prejudice." Researchers found that people subjected to harsh discipline in childhood suffer from anxiety and are intolerant of ambiguity. Not only do they view things in extremes, but they have paranoid fears, project hostility, and harbor strong beliefs in supernatural forces, among other traits.

Economic recessions, periods of war, and other disturbing conditions can cause stress on a large scale to a population. A study done by Sales[25] demonstrated that periods of national stress such as those we had in the 1930s can raise the level of anxiety for a population to the point where there are increases in social indicators of authoritarianism such as punitiveness against deviants, censorship, concerns for public morality, and apprehensions about threatening forces.

People in such a collective state of stress are certainly receptive to rumors that are hostile, and rumors of contamination and conspiracy fit very well into this prevailing mood. Such rumors give legitimacy to their sense of hostility, fear, and suspicion. To some suffering from such paranoia, a conspiracy rumor can indicate that their fears are well-founded, and a contamination rumor can demonstrate their conviction that one cannot trust anybody—even the most prestigious institutions.

Rumors That Produce Anxiety

There is another relationship between rumor and anxiety that needs to be discussed. Instead of reducing anxiety, many rumors tend to *increase* that state. The themes and content of rumor messages tend to be threatening and hostile and often allude to dangers or wrongdoings. Such stories can be thought of as stimulating anxiety in the average person and augmenting it in one who is already anxious.

Inasmuch as anxiety is looked upon as an unpleasant experience to be avoided, the question arises as to why anxious persons participate in an activity that can only increase their discomfort by raising their anxiety. One of the most versatile and problematic of the Freudian responses to this question is the idea of catharsis, which holds that sharing a frightening rumor would give vent to or purge the anxiety. Catharsis is part of a model in which it is presumed that one can expel drives, impulses, or motivational states from one's psychic system through symbolic experience—for example, watching a prize fight or a pornographic film gives one a vicarious experience which can lessen aggressiveness or the sex drive, respectively. This model is currently regarded as being unfounded. Allport and Postman believe that rumors have a cathartic effect on one's anxieties, so that one can reduce one's level of anxiety by hearing and/or telling a rumor.[26] However, other researchers have shown that hearing or telling rumors does not extinguish anxiety any more than viewing pictures of violence or eroticism reduces aggression or libidinal drives.[27]

The best explanation for the relationship between rumor participation and high anxiety, in my opinion, is that it provides justification for the feeling state of the rumor participant at the time. Rumors concerning a threatening and unpredictable world make a person's current disturbed and anxious state seem more appropriate and reasonable. One of the major theories dealing with how one strives for consistency between one's feelings and one's perception of certain events is Leon Festinger's work on cognitive dissonance.[28] The observation of rumor behavior in the previously mentioned earthquake cited by Prasad was a key item in the development of Festinger's particular theory. Festinger puzzled over the fact that people who were not in the earthquake-damaged area were engaged in circulating frightening rumors of disasters to come. "To the extent that any of these rumors were accepted and believed, they provided cognitive consonance with being afraid." He labeled these reports as "fear-justifying rumors."[29]

Fears are apprehensions regarding specific, recognized threats. Anxiety is an apprehension that is not related to anything known to the person. The two terms are often used interchangeably; in the case of the justification function of rumor, they operate in the same way. If a person is upset about such things as Satanism or earthquakes, rumors about them will vindicate his fears. However, if one does not have pinpointed fears but instead a general sense of uneasiness, rumors about the world falling apart and how "you can not trust anyone anymore" support this very bleak view of things. In a word, when you have anxiety and you hear upsetting rumors, you have brought your feelings and your experience into a kind of balance. Striving to keep things in balance is a major motivational variable in contemporary social psychology. Many rumor participants have both fears and anxieties which make them doubly receptive to the appropriate scary stories.

Rumor-prone Individuals

Some people are more apt to tell rumors than others because of their personal characteristics. As mentioned before, experiments have shown that anxiety is related to rumor activity. These studies were conducted by measuring a person's level of anxiety by using a psychological test, the Taylor Manifest Anxiety Scale.[30, 31] They showed that people who score high on the scale tell rumors more often. Thus an individual personality trait such as high anxiety can make a person more prone to relate rumors.

I referred to a formula presented by the pioneer investigators in rumors, Allport and Postman.[32] They said that the essential conditions for the transmission of a rumor are importance and ambiguity. A few years later, the Dutch psychologist Chorus[33] suggested that an individual characteristic which he called "critical sense" should be added to the formula. This critical sense, or perspicacity, is an individual feature which refers to the degree to which a person is willing to accept and pass on a rumor. The higher his critical sense, the less likely is a person to do so. (Buckner[34] has gone into more detail on this topic, and it will be dealt with in a future chapter.)

At first glance, this feature appears to be a form of personality trait, somewhat akin to persuadability, but Chorus considers it also volitional and situational. A person's involvement in a rumor may be related to his inherent gullibility, but it may also be related to how much he *wants* to participate in the rumor process, depending on his current attitude vis à vis the message. For instance, a person who is ordinarily perspicacious may be inclined to tell a story about an oil company if he has strong feelings against the oil company. On the other hand, an ordinarily noncritical person, who is loyal to the company where he works, will be reluctant to spread stories about that firm. There can be many dispositional factors involved in why rumors occur, but we can agree with Chorus that the volitional aspect plays a large part in determining the subjective quality of *relevance* for an individual.

Rumors may be functional in another sense. A major consideration in understanding the why of rumors is in the conscious motivation structure of the active rumor teller himself. An early observation about rumor behavior was made by Dr. Bernard Hart,[35] when he noted that rumor bearers have "the desire to figure as a person of distinction, to occupy the center of the stage, to have the eyes and ears of the neighbors directed admiringly toward us..." Peterson and Gist[36] say that relating inside information bearing on an issue of public concern places a person temporarily in a position of prestige. Spreading rumors is obviously a way of attracting attention, and a rumor teller who is cited as a source in the retelling may become a minor celebrity.

Since there are individual differences in the need for attention, there ought to be differing degrees to which people will be motivated to use rumors for this purpose. Schacter and Burdick[37] found that there is more rumor activity between acquaintances than between friends. Rosnow and Fine's tracking of the "death of Paul McCartney" allegation shows that the only individual difference to amount to anything between rumormongers and "dead-enders" is popularity. The former "were less popular, they dated less often, and got together with friends less frequently than non-rumormongers."[38] Loners standing on the social fringe and looking for more acceptance must find the motivation for telling a rumor to be very strong.

Endnotes

1. Brunvand, Jan, *The Vanishing Hitchhiker: American Urban Legends and Their Meanings* (New York: W.W. Norton & Co., Inc., 1979).

2. Tybout, Alice M., Bobby J. Calder, and Brian Sternthal, "Using Information Processing Theory to Design Marketing Strategies," *Journal of Marketing Research*, vol. 18, no. 1 (1981), pp. 73-86.
3. Allport, Gordon, and Leo Postman, *The Psychology of Rumor* (New York: Henry Holt and Co., 1946), p. 180.
4. Allport and Postman, *op. cit.*, p. 431.
5. Rosnow, Ralph, "Psychology of Rumor Reconsidered," *Psychological Bulletin*, vol. 6 (1980), pp. 578-591.
6. Volkart, Edmund H., *Social Behavior and Personality: Contributions of W.I. Thomas to Theory and Social Research* (New York: Social Science Research Council, 1951).
7. Rosnow, Ralph, and Gary Fine, *Rumor and Gossip* (New York: Elsevier, 1976).
8. Shibutani, Tomatso, *Improvised News* (Indianapolis: Bobbs-Merrill, 1966).
9. Bauer, Raymond, and David Gleicher, "Word of Mouth Communication in the Soviet Union," *Public Opinion Quarterley*, vol. 17, no. 3 (1953), pp. 299-310.
10. Prasad, Jamuna, "A Comparative Study of Rumors and Reports on Earthquakes," *British Journal of Psychology*, vol. 26 (1935), pp. 1-15.
11. Smelser, Neal, *Theory of Collective Behavior* (New York: Free Press, 1962).
12. Shibutani, *op. cit.*, p. 133.
13. Schacter, Stanley, and Harvey Burdick, "A Field Experiment on Rumor Transmission and Distortion," *Journal of Abnormal and Social Psychology*, vol. 50 (1955), pp. 363-371.
14. Schacter and Burdick, *op. cit.*, p. 365.
15. Schacter and Burdick, *op. cit.*, pp. 365-366.
16. Sherif, Mazafer, *Group Conflict and Co-operation: Their Social Psychology* (London: Routledge & Kegan Paul, 1967).
17. Knopf, Terry, *Rumors, Race and Riots* (New Brunswick, New Jersey: Transaction Books, 1975), p. 164.
18. Jackson, Wesley, "Please Don't Keep Those Cards and Letters Coming," *New Orleans Times-Picayune/States-Item* (Jan. 22, 1983), Sec. 4, p. 2.
19. Miller, Neal, and John Dollard, *Social Learning and Imitation* (New Haven: Yale University Press, 1941).
20. Miller, Neal and John Dollard, *op. cit.*
21. Anthony, Susan, "Anxiety and Rumor," *Journal of Social Psychology*, vol. 89 (1973), pp. 91-98.
22. Jaeger, Marianne, Susan Anthony, and Ralph Rosnow, "Who Hears What from Whom and with What Effect: A Study of Rumor," *Personality and Social Psychology Bulletin*, vol. 6 (1980), pp. 473-478.
23. Rosnow, Ralph, "Psychology of Rumor Reconsidered," *Psychological Bulletin*, vol. 87, no. 2 (1980), pp. 578-591.
24. Adorno, Theodore W., Else Frenkel-Brunswick, Daniel J. Levinson, and R.N. Sanford, *The Authoritarian Personality* (New York, Harper & Row, 1950).
25. Sales, Stephen M, "Threat as a Factor in Authoritarianism," *Journal of*

Personality and Social Psychology, vol. 28 (1973), pp. 44-57.

26. Allport and Postman, *op. cit.*
27. Anthony, *op. cit.*
28. Festinger, Leon, *A Theory of Cognitive Dissonance* (Stanford Calif.: Stanford University Press, 1957).
29. Festinger, *op. cit.,* p. 238.
30. Anthony, *op. cit.*
31. Jaeger, *op. cit.*
32. Allport and Postman, *op. cit.*
33. Chorus, A., "The Basic Law of Rumor," *Journal of Abnormal and Social Psychology,* vol. 48 (1953), pp. 313-314.
34. Buckner, H. Taylor, "A Theory of Rumor Transmission," *Public Opinion Quarterley,* vol. 29 (1965), pp. 54-70.
35. Hart, Bernard, *Psychopathology, Its Development and Place in Medicine* (Cambridge England: The University Press, 1929), p. 121.
36. Peterson and Gist, *op. cit.*
37. Schacter and Burdick, *op. cit.*
38. Rosnow and Fine, *op. cit.,* pp. 74-75.

Chapter Four

CONTEMPORARY COMMERCIAL RUMORS, PART I: CONSPIRACY THEMES

In this chapter and the next we shall analyze some recent commercial rumors. They will be examined according to the two categories into which these rumors fall, with this chapter taking up conspiracy rumors and Chapter 5 dealing with contamination rumors. Descriptions of the cases will be presented first, providing an overview of the category, followed by analysis and discussion of the rumor events.

Conspiracy rumors are those in which the allegation connects a political, religious, or other ideological movement with a visible target: a successful commercial enterprise. The carriers of the rumor are members of a population who feel that the movement is undesirable and threatening. The point of the message concerns the movement cited in the charge. The corporate target serves to emphasize the extent and magnitude of the threat. The following examples of recent conspiracy rumors are presented for analysis and as a basis of generalizations.

Procter & Gamble and the Man in the Moon

The Procter & Gamble experience with rumors is probably the longest, most widely publicized, most expensive confrontation with rumor of any in the marketplace. The case actually involves two messages: one concerning Procter & Gamble's connection with the Unification Church of the Reverend Sun Myung Moon, and the other concerning the Church of Satan. (This double hitting of Procter & Gamble constitutes a convergent process. If you take into account the McDonald's Satan rumor, combined with Procter & Gamble's Satan rumor, there is also a divergent process.) The Moonie-Satan convergence had a strange dual career in the early phase of the Procter & Gamble case. I became aware of both rumors simultaneously. On March 26 the *Wall Street Journal*[1] had an article about some people in Minnesota who were upset over alleged "Moonie ownership of Procter & Gamble." After making the charge, it continued:

> *Then a few weeks ago they started again. The calls came from towns like Gaylord, Lafayette, and Brownton, in an area 80 miles southwest of Minneapolis–St. Paul.*
>
> *Then the* Potpourri, *a monthly newsletter for employees at the Lakeview Home, a nursing home in Gaylord, carried a squib from an employee that said the Moon church owned P & G. That promoted the* Lafayette-Nicollet Ledger *to prepare an editorial favorably inclined toward a boycott of P & G products. Before it ran, however, the paper checked with P & G. The editorial that later appeared chided residents for spreading the rumor and said, "If you are asked to participate in a product boycott, check your sources of information first. It is easy to allow rumors to circulate."*
>
> *Next month's* Potpourri *will retract the takeover item, said Larry Schulz, administrator of the nursing home and of Gaylord Community Hospital.*

On the same day the *Washington Post*[2] had an article on its business page written "Special to the *Washington Post*" and datelined Minneapolis. It dealt with the rumor that "Sun Myung Moon and his followers control the company and are skimming off 75 % of its profits," but added that a more recent rumor was that "the crescent moon-faced logo with a cluster of stars is a symbol of witchcraft, satan, or both." The article continued,

> *This week, Procter & Gamble denied the current witch-devil version, a separate and opposite rumor. The* Minneapolis Tribune *traced one of the sources of the occult tale to Paul Martin, director of the high school club division of the Youth for Christ Office in Willmar, Minn.*

According to Martin, the Procter & Gamble logo is a symbol associated with witchcraft and Satan, and he offered as evidence his belief it could be found on a satanic church in St. Paul. This was a reference to a plain crescent moon on the Gnostica Bookstore, which denied any connections with P & G, devils, or witches.

Martin said the person who brought the logo story to Willmar was Jim Peters, a St. Paul fundamentalist and crusader against rock music. Peters said his main target was rock music, and he mentioned the logo only in passing in his twice-a-month "music seminars" in Minnesota. He said his main complaint is that P & G sponsored TV programs containing sex and profanity.

Peters said he wasn't accusing the company of witchcraft or of sponsoring Satan, but said his Zion Christian Life Center wanted to know "what's going on," and the company had replied to inquiries with only a "standard form letter."

He said he found an exact copy of the logo, identified as a sign for a witches coven, in a book by E.A. Wallis Duge called Amulets and Superstitions.

The Minneapolis Tribune said two of its reporters read the book cover-to-cover and could not find the reference.

Cathy Gilbert,[3] who worked on the rumor assignment for Procter & Gamble, said the problems with the logo started to appear in early 1979, when their office received inquiries from three reporters and six customers in Florida about Moonie ownership. (The Unification Church bought property in Florida about that time.) During the rest of 1979, Procter & Gamble received half a dozen calls about the Moonies from around the country. From January through March of 1980, they received 33 calls about witchcraft and/or the Church of Satan. One of the spreaders of the latter tale was a Minnesota minister named Wynn Worley, who admitted telling people that the Procter & Gamble logo symbolized witchcraft. Despite contrary arguments from the Cincinnati office of Procter & Gamble, he remained adamant. He maintained that Procter & Gamble might not be in cahoots with the devil, but that—whether they knew it or not—their trademark stood for what he said it stood for.

During 1980 the cards and letters kept coming in, a couple of hundred a month. Sometimes they connected the logo with Satanism; somewhat more often they connected it with the Moonies. The Satan-witchcraft version faded somewhat as the year passed, while the Moonie version came into ascendance.

Satan Pulls Ahead

Then, in October of 1981, the rumor became a crisis. In the
Pacific Northwest, it became more specific and elaborate. It
was a rerun of the first McDonald's rumor, complete with the
Phil Donahue Show as the attributed source. The owner of
Procter & Gamble supposedly appeared on the show and
admitted that he contributed 20 percent of the company's
earnings to the Church of Satan. A Faustian twist was given
some versions with the claim that the owner of Procter &
Gamble had admitted making a pact with the Devil to help him
become successful in return for which he would pay him part of
the company's profits. Not surprisingly, the actual head of
Procter & Gamble was not identified; very few people know
who he is, and he has never been on television or written a book
extolling his achievements. This embellished rumor moved
quickly to the Midwest and the South, with the attributed
source tending to be most often the *Phil Donahue Show*, but
sometimes *Merv Griffin*, or *60 minutes*.

By spring of 1982 the rumor was spreading like brushfire in
Texas, Oklahoma, and the Southeast Bible Belt. Exhortations
were made from pulpits, and calls for boycotts hit the church
newsletter network and fanned out. The church newsletters
began to offer similar formats for exposing the Satan connection. Usually, they would reprint an anonymous letter received
at the church which would tell of the events of *Donahue, Merv
Griffin*, or *60 Minutes* (see Exhibit 4-1). Later versions had this
added touch: The Procter & Gamble logo was redrawn to show
the figure 666—the sign of the Beast according to the Book of
Revelation (see Exhibit 4-2). The hidden demonic code number
was derived from the original design by playing "connect the
dots" with the thirteen stars and drawing lines between them to
form the three-digit code. It was also pointed out that a close
look at the mirror image of the curls on the man in the moon
depicted three "6's." Of course, as in the McDonald's case, the
items in the newsletters were copied by other church newsletter
editors and the spread was multiplicative.

Although sales representatives spent much of their time trying to convince retailers that the company was not connected
with the Devil, they were frequently turned away or warned
that their products were being returned. Procter & Gamble

EDITOR: Recently I received a copy of the following copy of the following letter (sic). After reading it I felt a need to let other people know this information. The letter reads as follows:

IN GOD WE TRUST

Recently on the Merv Griffin talk show a group of cults were brought to the attention of the public. Among these appeared the owner of the Procter and Gamble Corporation. He said that as long as the gays and the cults have come out of the closet, he was going to do it too. He also said that he told Satan that if he would help him to prosper, that he would give him his heart and soul when he died. He gives Satan all the credit for his riches.

So, would you please take copies of this letter and the list of his products and pass them out so Christians will not give him any more business or money. Use what you have, but buy no more. All of these products have a satanic insignia on them. It is a quarter moon shape and has a three 6's (666) and ram's horns, which is the anti-Christ symbol. (See illustration)

Some of the products are: Deodorant—Sure and Secret; Shampoo—Prell, Head and Shoulders; Toothpaste—Crest; Lotion—Wondra; Mouthwash—Scope; Permanents—Lilt; Toilet Tissue—Charmin, Bounty; Washing Products—Bounce, Downy, Biz, Mr. Clean, Joy, Dawn, Ivory, Camay, Bold, and Tide.

After reading this letter I looked on the labels of some of the products listed that I had in my home. And there I found the anti-Christ symbol (as pictured) although it was reduced to a very small size which you probably would not recognize if you had not read this letter.

Several people asked me if this was true. I can't say for sure, but why would the owner of Procter and Gamble let this symbol stay on all of his products if it were not true.

I honestly believe that any God-fearing Christian presented with this information cannot, with good conscience, buy any more of these items. There are so many products on the market today that I feel certain that there are replacement products for all of them.

I hope that before you buy any old or new product that you will check the label for this symbol. And if the anti-Christ insignia appears on the label that you will put it back on the shelf and find a replacement that lacks the symbol.

Thank you,

A Concerned Christian

(Name withheld by request)

Exhibit 4-1   Example of the kind of letter being sent to newspapers

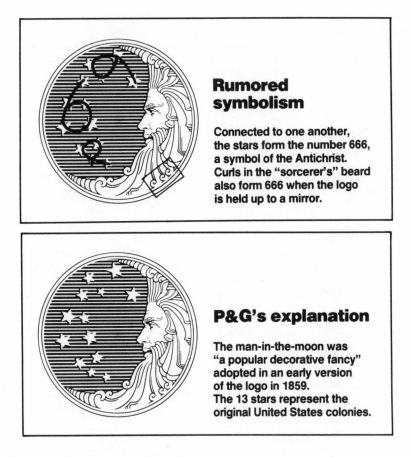

Exhibit 4-2   Procter & Gamble logotype. (Source: *Advertising Age,*
August 9, 1982.)

motor vehicles became targets of vandalism. The whole scene
began to take on the eerie aspects of a Flannery O'Connor short
story. Inquiries regarding the connection with the Church of
Satan rose to 500 per day; four extra staff members were hired
just to answer the phones. Procter & Gamble did not feel that
profits were being hurt, but the rumor and its effects were
becoming a colossal nuisance.

Fundamentalist church leaders such as Jerry Falwell and
Donald Wildmon were deluged with inquiries, and they asked
Procter & Gamble what they could do to combat the stories.
(The working relationship between Procter & Gamble and the
Moral Majority was a good one, because that company had

been one of the first to cooperate with the Moral Majority's requests regarding television programming.) They asked Procter & Gamble to supply them with pamphlets, letters, and literature—anything they could mail back in response to the questions. In June Procter & Gamble solicited and obtained statements from these church leaders and others to support them in the fight against the rumor. Letters with statements and disclaimers were sent to 48,000 Southern churches. There were press releases with statements from the Reverends Falwell, Graham, and Wildmon (see Exhibits 4-3, 4-4, 4-5). "Dear Ann" and "Dear Abby" also became involved (see Exhibit 4-6). *Christianity Today* wrote an editorial (see Exhibit 4-7).

As Cathy Gilbert said, "The company struggled with that decision for a long time. You know we were afraid to 'go public,' thinking it would add fuel to fire and alert people who had never even heard about it."[4] However, the inquiries about the rumor reached a point where Procter & Gamble president, John G. Smale, who had the reputation of injecting new aggressiveness into the organization, told the public relations department to forget the earlier cautious policy. On June 10 the department presented its recommendation to Mr. Smale. William Dobson of the public relations department was quoted as saying in a *New York Times* interview, "It was essential to go on the offensive."[5]

On July 1, 1982, the public relations office of Procter & Gamble held a press conference to announce that they had decided to make an open, all-out fight against the Satan rumor. Their campaign was three-pronged: mass mailings to churches, denials to the media, and lawsuits against several individuals who had been identified as spreading the rumor. The purpose of the lawsuits, of course, was to call public attention to the company's strong stand against the rumor, not necessarily to obtain legal redress.

By the end of July the calls about the rumors fell off sharply to about 7,000 per month. In September they were down to 1,000, and by spring of 1983 there were only a couple of hundred calls a month. The *New York Times* gave a wind-up story in the spring of 1983:[6]

> *Most lawsuits, filed against seven individuals believed to have spread the rumors, have been resolved. One, against an Atlanta weatherman and lay minister, was settled when he made a public*

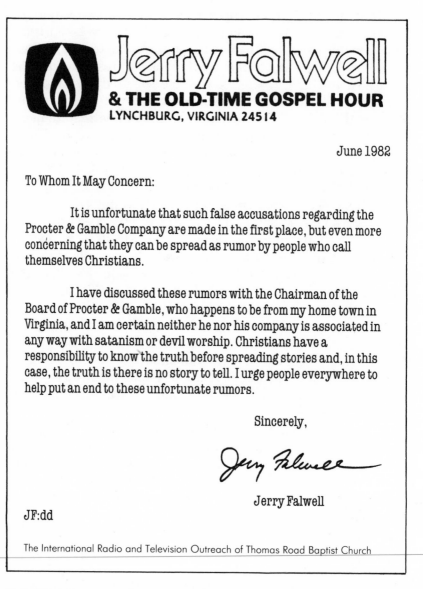

& THE OLD-TIME GOSPEL HOUR
LYNCHBURG, VIRGINIA 24514

June 1982

To Whom It May Concern:

It is unfortunate that such false accusations regarding the Procter & Gamble Company are made in the first place, but even more concerning that they can be spread as rumor by people who call themselves Christians.

I have discussed these rumors with the Chairman of the Board of Procter & Gamble, who happens to be from my home town in Virginia, and I am certain neither he nor his company is associated in any way with satanism or devil worship. Christians have a responsibility to know the truth before spreading stories and, in this case, the truth is there is no story to tell. I urge people everywhere to help put an end to these unfortunate rumors.

Sincerely,

Jerry Falwell

JF:dd

The International Radio and Television Outreach of Thomas Road Baptist Church

Exhibit 4-3

apology. *Most others, against distributors of competing household products, ended in similar consent decrees. But charges against Linda Moore, an independent Amway dealer, are still pending.*

Satan's effect on Procter's business is difficult to gauge. Sales and earnings have improved since 1980, and earnings for the quarter ended last September 30 rose 15.2 percent, but the

BILLY GRAHAM

July 31, 1982

Unfounded rumors have been spread that the Procter &
Gamble Company has some connection to devil worship.

Unfortunately, some of these false accusations have
been spread in various churches.

These rumors claim that the Procter & Gamble
100-year-old trademark with its famous moon and 13
stars representing the 13 colonies has something to
do with the supporting of satanism and devil worship.
I have found this to be absolutely false. I urge
Christians everywhere to reject these false rumors
and to be reminded that it is a sin to "bear false
witness."

Billy Graham

Exhibit 4-4

*company says last summer's publicity and legal campaign cost
millions. "It has certainly been a major distraction to our business," said Mrs. Ulrey. (A spokesperson who was interviewed.)*

As of this writing, the Moonie rumor has not returned, but the
Satan rumor has been revived. On the morning of October 24,
1984, there was mention on CBS network radio news that Procter & Gamble was again being victimized by the rumor that it is
affiliated with the Church of Satan. That same day, a letter to
Ann Landers was published in the New Orleans daily newspaper[7] reaffirming that the problem was back (see Exhibit 4-8).
And the next day, the *Wall Street Journal* had a side-bar to a
P & G sales story which briefly described the problem:[8]

Procter & Gamble
Rumor Not True

The National Federation for Decency has received several calls concerning a supposed program in which an official for Procter & Gamble said his company gave money to the church of satan. We have checked this out to the best of our ability and have not been able to find anyone who actually saw the program. It is a rumor which began on the West Coast and is moving to the east. We have contacted P&G about the rumor and desire to take this method to let you know that it is nothing more than a rumor.

Please tell anyone who mentions this rumor to you that it is only a rumor and has no basis of fact.

While we feel companies should be held accountable for the programs they decide to help sponsor, we also feel that unfounded rumors should be identified and treated as such.

Barry M. Smyth, with the public affairs division of P&G, wrote us: "A company that undertakes sole sponsorship of programs such as Jesus of Nazareth and Peter and Paul is about as far away from devil worship as you can get."

Mr. Smyth continues: "Harley Procter, the son of one of our cofounders, came up with the name Ivory as a result of reading Psalm 45 in church one Sunday in 1878: 'All my garments smell of myrrh and aloes and cassia, out of the ivory palaces whereby they have made thee glad'."

P&G does not give money to the church of satan.

March 30, 1982

Chrm. Owen Butler
Procter & Gamble Company
Post Office Box 599
Cincinnati, Ohio 45201

Dear Mr. Butler:

We have received many calls in our office concerning the validity of a rumor that Procter & Gamble gives part of their money to the church of satan. In all cases, we have told those who asked that the rumor simply was not true.

To further help stop this vicious, untrue rumor we printed an article in our April NFD INFORMER about the rumor. This edition of our paper was mailed to approximately 150,000 churches in addition to our regular subscribers.

As you know we have had disagreement with Procter & Gamble on some occasions in the past and no doubt will have some disagreement with Procter & Gamble in the future. However, disagreement should be based on fact, not rumor.

I hope that the article in our paper will help stop this awful rumor. You have my permission to use this letter in any way you desire. I ask my fellow ministers and others in position of influence to inform their people that the rumor is untrue and for those individuals to continue using your fine products as they have in the past.

Although it will be of no consolation to you, this rumor first started about two years ago. At that time it was in reference to a large restaurant chain. Somewhere along the way Procter & Gamble replaced that chain as the culprit. Other than that the rumor is identical to its original beginnings.

If I can help further in any way in this matter, please feel free to contact me. I will be happy to do whatever I can.

Sincerely,

Donald E. Wildmon

Donald E. Wildmon
Executive Director, NFD
Chairman, Coalition for Better Television   DEW/wed

Exhibit 4-5   Reprinted April 1982 on front page of *NFD Informer*

DEAR ANN LANDERS: Please tell your millions of readers the real truth about Procter & Gamble's tie-in with the Moonies and the Unification Church.

A friend of mine told me that her cousin saw a high-up executive of Procter & Gamble on the ABC news-magazine "20/20" and he said that his company had made a pact with the Moonies, who assured them that if they used the Moonie symbol on all their products, their business would prosper. In return, Procter & Gamble would give Rev. Sun Myung Moon a huge sum of money for protecting them against the devil.

I told my cousin it sounded like a lot of baloney. She said she doubted it, too, until she looked at a box of detergent put out by P&G and there was the trademark — the moon and stars she said represented the Moonies.

Clear this up once and for all, Ann. If you say it, the American people will believe it. — Reader in Tennessee

DEAR TENNESSEE — and readers in the other 49 states and Canada who wrote to me about this: The facts are as follows:

Procter & Gamble has been plagued by this off-the-wall rumor for more than two years and there is not a shred of truth to it. The trademark featuring the man-in-the-moon against a field of 13 stars was designed in 1850. It was first used as an identifying mark on a crate of candles. The 13 stars represent the original colonies.

In July, Procter & Gamble announced that it is taking legal action to stop the spread of rumors that have mushroomed into a campaign to boycott P&G products. Suits have been filed against individuals in Atlanta, Ga., and Pensacola, Fla., for making statements or distributing false and malicious literature.

Stay tuned. It should be fascinating to hear the testimony of people who seem to have nothing better to do than circulate lies.

DEAR ABBY: I just received a mimeographed letter in the mail telling me not to buy products made by Procter & Gamble. It was signed, "A Good Christian." It said the Procter & Gamble Co. supports a religious cult dedicated to witchcraft and the devil. As proof, I was sent a picture of the P&G trademark insignia — a man's face in a half-moon with 13 stars, a symbol of Satan.

The letter stated that the owner of Procter & Gamble appeared on "The Merv Griffin Show" and also on "Donahue," saying he owed his success to "Satan"!

Abby, can you find out if the Procter & Gamble Co. has any connection with Satan and witchcraft, because if it has, I am not buying any more of its products. — NEEDS TO KNOW IN OHIO

DEAR NEEDS: Letters such as the one you received have been circulated through the U.S. for the last two years, and there is not a shred of truth in the rumor that P&G is connected with Satan, witchcraft or the devil.

Furthermore, neither Merv Griffin nor Phil Donahue has had anyone from Procter & Gamble on their shows, but this rumor has been so widespread that both Griffin and Donahue have had to send out form letters to deny this false accusation.

Some of the nation's most respected Christian religious leaders have issued public statements in an effort to put an end to this vicious campaign. They include the Rev. Jerry Falwell; the Rev. Jimmy Draper, president of the Southern Baptist Convention; the Rev. Donald E. Wildmon, Methodist minister and executive of the National Federation for Decency; Bishop Emerson Colaw, United Methodist Church; and the Rev. William C. Black, bishop of the Episcopal diocese of Southern Ohio.

All "good Christians" who have specific information about anyone distributing this propaganda should write to: Procter & Gamble, P.O. Box 599, Department D.A., Cincinnati, Ohio 45201. Please include your name, address and telephone number.

Exhibit 4-6 (Source: *New Orleans Times–Picayune/States Item,* September 6, 1982 and August 3, 1982.)

The Terrible Truth about that Procter and Gamble Symbol

It's not Satanic; the Moonies don't own the company.

Apparently Christians easily forget that gossip is a sin, and some of America's largest marketing firms are plagued by the consequences.

For the second time in as many years, Procter and Gamble Company, the consumer product manufacturing giant, has been targeted by a campaign of unfounded rumor. The current wave, which began last October, charges that P & G actively promotes Satanism. It is circulating in the Pacific coastal states and typically ·alleges that a P & G executive appeared on either the Phil Donahue or the Merv Griffin television talk show and publicly linked P & G with promotion of Satanism.

Statements have been issued by spokesmen for both the Donahue and Griffin programs to deny that they had ever interviewed a P & G official.

The tenuous basis for the rumor is apparently the P & G corporate symbol: a man-in-the-moon profile and 13 stars. The rumor mongers claim this is a sorcerer's head and that the number of stars is of significance in Satan worship. Actually, according to P & G spokeswoman Kathy Gilbert, the 13 stars were chosen in the 1850s to represent the original colonies, and the man-in-the-moon was tossed in by William Procter and James Gamble because it caught their fancy. The man-in-the-moon profile was a fad at the time—much as the happy face is today.

A year earlier, the Cincinnati, Ohio–based P & G was subjected to a spate of rumors, largely from the upper Midwest, alleging that the firm had been bought out by Sun Myung Moon's Unification Church. P & G, which markets products such as Folger's coffee, Ivory soap, Head & Shoulders shampoo, and Pampers disposable diapers, has never been approached by

The P&G corporate logo, which first evolved in 1851. At lower left is the 1882 version, the one registered in the U.S. Patent Office, and at right, the 1920 model.

the Moonies.

In both cases, Gilbert said, the inquiries came from individuals who typically stated that they "heard it at their church over the weekend." She observed that they referred to "fundamentalist-type churches," and that a few of the churches had attempted to organize boycotts of P & G products.

Sales have not been perceptibly affected by the rash of rumors, but P & G officials, taking no chances, have spent several hundred dollars to combat the slander. "It's a lot cheaper to fight the rumors than it is to have the corporate symbol redesigned," said another company spokesperson. ☐

Exhibit 4-7 (Source: *Christianity Today,* April 9, 1982)

It's bad enough to have to report a drop in earnings; Procter &
Gamble Co. also has to convince people it isn't giving money to
the devil.
  The idea that the company's "man in the moon" trademark is
linked to the Church of Satan—a rumor that first reared its horns
in 1981—has returned to plague P & G.
  The company has answered 3,000 calls this month from people
who believe that P & G is in league with the devil. More speci-
fically, the callers say, they've been told that the company's chief
executive officer, John Smale, appeared on "60 Minutes" or
"Good Morning, America" or the "Phil Donahue Show," that he
is a member of the Church of Satan, that the company contributes
money to the church and that "there aren't enough Christians in
the world to stop it." Callers also say they've been urged to boy-
cott P & G products.

That week's issue of *Advertising Age* had a front page story,
"Rumor returns to bedevil P & G." The article reported
increases in inquiries about the Satan connection to about 1000
in September and to 3000 in October.[9]
A call to Bill Dobson at P & G revealed that, indeed, they did
"have a problem." Although it was not as bad as two years
previous, they wanted to deal with it locally before it spread
further. He said they were sending out mailings describing the
history of the logo, a disclaimer to the *Phil Donahue Show*
component of the story and the old letters from evangelist Billy
Graham and Jerry Falwell. The irony of the latter move is that
the trouble seemed to be coming not from fundamentalists this
time but from Catholics. In areas such as western Pennsylvania, Buffalo, Cleveland, Chicago, and Nebraska, nuns and
priests were putting notices in newsletters and church bulletins, urging their students to go home and tell their parents to
boycott P & G products because the president of the company
said that there weren't enough Christians "to affect his alliance
with the Church of Satan."[10] Later, *The Wall Street Journal* did
a feature story on the problem and presented the case of Sister
Domitilla:[11]

Sister Domitilla Drobnsk, the principal of St. Anthony's element-
ary school in this mining town east of Pittsburgh, didn't know who
put the leaflet in her mailbox six weeks ago. But she knew what
she had to do when she got it.
  The leaflet told how the president of Procter & Gamble Co. had
appeared on the Phil Donahue Show *to declare his company's*
support for the Church of Satan. And it showed a magnified

DEAR ANN LANDERS: Please clarify the rumors that are running rampant concerning a recent representative of Procter & Gamble who was supposedly on the *Phil Donahue Show* discussing P&G's relationship with a satanic church.

Since I am not a TV viewer during the daytime but am a big user of P&G products, I would like to get to the bottom of this.

The P&G representative was said to have made some comments about there not being enough Christians left in this country to concern themselves with a boycott of P&G products. I have never heard of this so-called Satan Church, but with our country's freedom of religion I would not be surprised at what kind of hocus-pocus is out there. Will you please chase down the facts?

Not Easily Bamboozled in Colorado

DEAR BOOZLED: Is that wild story loose again? I thought it was buried two years ago.

There is absolutely no connection between Procter & Gamble and any church. No P&G representative appeared on the *Phil Donahue Show*. It's pure malarkey. Funny how a lie can travel halfway 'round the world before the truth can get its shoelaces tied.

Exhibit 4-8   (Source: *New Orleans Times-Picayune/States Item,* October 25, 1984)

picture of P & G's "man in the moon" trademark, which it said was the sign of Satan.

So Sister Domitilla made copies of the leaflet and added a note of her own, urging a boycott of such familiar P & G products as Crest toothpaste, Tide detergent, and Ivory soap. She sent 70 copies home with St. Anthony's students. "I thought I was going to fight for social justice," she says.

When describing her reaction to the contents of the accusation, Sister Domitilla said:[12]

"That shocked me," Sister Domitilla recalls. She wanted everybody "to know what people are thinking about us Christians. We have to be stronger in our faith." So she signed her name to a note urging other Christians to "prove we do make a difference." And the word began to spread.

There was a noticeable transformation of the message each time P & G was plagued. The first version was a vague claim that the logo was a witchcraft symbol. The second version, a couple of years later, was a specific retread of the old McDonald's allegation that the president of the corporation appeared on the *Phil Donahue Show*, etc. As this series made the rounds, however, it was obvious to most people how foolish it would be for a corporation official to confess such a thing on national television and thereby jeopardize his business. A very likely rejoinder to that suggestion was the added kicker about the president commenting on the inability of a few disinterested Christians to have any effect. This taunt seemed to have considerable capacity to create outrage among Christians who heard it.

What caused a resurgence of P & G's problem? Nothing can be proved, but some observation and conjectures are appropriate. The original rumor problem had been around a long time, and during that period sparks had been allowed to scatter far and wide. When the public relations people decided to douse the conflagration, there were areas around the country they could not reach, and the rumor lay smoldering. Catholic nuns and some priests, for example, had not been party to the campaign directed at fundamentalist congregations in the previous couple of years. Because they have a moderately reclusive lifestyle, they probably were untouched by the national media blitz that P & G launched in the summer of 1982.

As has been pointed out, anxiety brought about by frustration and stress increases the likelihood of rumor activity. In the 1984 election campaign, Catholics often found themselves in an adversarial position concerning abortion, prayer, and the role of religion in politics generally. They may have felt under attack and threatened. Also, unemployment and economic depression seemed to characterize the regions that were the centers of the rumor activity:[13]

> *The economy of Vandergrift, Father Weber explains, has been ravaged by the closings of a foundry and of the U.S. Steel plant that sits, now eerily silent, at the head of the main street into town. "So many people have lost their jobs," he says, "and so many are upset by (the idea of) nuclear war. To them, almost anything can happen." In searching for explanations, he adds, "a lot can get to the point where they think they're being punished. It's easier to blame it on the devil."*

Not the least of the considerations for explaining the persistence and repeated emergence of the rumor is the message itself. It has all the ingredients of a successful rumor: It is attention-getting and dramatic—imagine the excitement of Christians being asked to rally against Satan! It legitimates a cosmology for a large number of people, justifies their fears and explains their anxieties. Jolie Solomon of *The Wall Street Journal* was aware of the message's appeal:[14]

> *But some who believe the rumor are loath to give it up—whatever the evidence—as Virginia Meaves recently found out. Mrs. Meaves ran the Satanism story in* Wisconsin Report, *the 6,000-circulation weekly newspaper she edits in suburban Milwaukee. (The paper, which isn't affiliated with any church, usually reports on such issues as abortion and government regulation.) When P & G's staffers called her to demand a retraction, she complied, only to rile some readers. "People are disappointed," Mrs. Meaves says. "They get mad at me. They'd like to send out thousands of fliers."*

On April 24, 1985, Procter & Gamble announced its intention to remove the logotype from its products' packages. The decision was made after a severe flare-up of the rumor early in 1985, resulting in thousands of phone calls to the company. Drawing the line, however, management said that the logo would be retained on company letterhead and publications. It remains to be seen whether this step will finally end the long-persisting saga of commercial hearsay.

Another Half-Baked Moonie Episode[15]

Although the Moonie rumor concerning Procter & Gamble disappeared, the tenacious story acquired a diversionary existence by becoming attached to yet another corporation, Entenmann's, a wholesale bakery operation concentrated mainly in the eastern United States. Their products are delivered fresh by trucks to retail food outlets. A highly successful operation and a prominent enterprise, it was founded in 1948 and is now the world's largest producer of fresh bakery products. In 1978 it was purchased by Warner-Lambert Corporation (it has since been sold to General Foods), and all advertising material, posters, pastry-boxes, and the like stated, "A wholly owned subsidiary of Warner-Lambert." Rumormongers converted the "wholly" to "holy" in their stories in order to strengthen their claim about the connection with the Unification Church.

The accusation about Moonie ownership was a much more serious problem for Entenmann's Bakery than it was for Procter & Gamble. Walter Weglein, manager of consumer communications at Warner-Lambert, says the questions began coming from New Jersey during the summer of 1979. A letter to the *New York Daily News* asked about Moonie ownership. The next month there were 150 reported consumer complaints to retail managers about their carrying Entenmann's products.

Early in 1980 the activity increased. This time it was not fundamentalist bible-pounding people but upper-middle-class Protestant church members who were agitating. Suburban homemakers from Long Island, Connecticut, and New Jersey would stand up at Sunday services to announce that Entenmann's "is owned by the Moonies" and call for everyone to refrain from buying their baked goods "even if they are the best around."

Similar exhortations appeared in church bulletins, letters to the editor, and phone calls to radio shows. Entenmann's decided to respond by communicating with the clergy, who were the influential, respected opinion leaders of those who were spreading the story. Some 8,200 letters were sent out to clergy. This tactic appeared to be somewhat successful, until the television program *Saturday Night Live* had a brief item of humor in one of its television news take-offs. It went something like, "There's a rumor that Entenmann's Bakery has been taken over by the Moonies. Entenmann's denies it, but how come their gingerbread men wear braids, have blank looks on their faces, and ask for money?" The results of the original telecast were not so bad, but the various local rebroadcasts of the program brought in letters from all over the country. Each time there was a new broadcast, there would be a resurgence of the rumor problem. Next, the Unification Church actually bought property in Westchester County (New York), and the rumors there became enough of a problem that Walter Weglein initiated an advertising campaign to counter it. He took out ads in Long Island newspapers and gave copies to their store outlets. As a result, the problem seemed to quiet down in that area.

Boston TV Party

In 1981 things became worse for Entenmann's. Rumors flourished in Boston when the Moonies bought into several phases of the fishing and fish-processing industry in Gloucester. The situation was more serious than it had been anywhere, as rumors spread from church-goers to the general public. The rumormongers now accompanied the tale with a stated resolve to stop buying any Entenmann's products. Distributors and salespeople were confronted with accusations and epithets, and one driver was physically assaulted by an irate customer in a store.

In October of 1981, Walter Weglein called me and said that he had talked with Robert Entenmann and with his own public relations staff and that he had decided to deal with the problem forthrightly. He asked me to work with him and the Boston public relations firm Agnew, Carter, McCarthy, Inc. in putting together a media campaign in the Boston area. A major press conference was called in Boston on November 9th. Radio interviews and television appearances were made for several days. Robert Entenmann talked about the history and current status of the company and about the inaccuracy and unfairness of the Moonie rumor specifically, while I talked about rumors generally. (In retrospect, the fact that I was along seemed to help overcome the reluctance of some radio and television stations to give Entenmann's free promotional time; they were more willing to do a piece on the psychology of rumor with

Entenmann's as an example.) The story got into local and national media. The *Boston Globe*[16] ran the following item:

> Robert Entenmann said he came to town yesterday because he is *"fighting mad"* but doesn't know who to fight.
>
> His enemy is the rumor mill.
>
> For the past two years, Entenmann's Bakery has been trying to kill the tale that it is owned by the Unification Church of the Rev. Sun Myung Moon, popularly known as *"Moonies."* The company has found that tall tales do not die or even fade away— they just persist.
>
> *"Two years ago we heard a rumor that the Unification Church had bought the bakery and we all laughed,"* Entenmann told reporters at the Ritz-Carlton. *"Well, it's not funny anymore."*
>
> The chairman of the 83-year-old family business, which was purchased in 1978 by Warner-Lambert Co., said he held his first news conference on the subject in Boston because the rumor was strongest in New England. He said the story was hurting sales, causing salesmen and truck drivers to be harassed—one driver was knocked down by a customer in a store in Connecticut—and generally chipping away at the company's reputation.
>
> *"Our reputation has spread by word of mouth,"* he said, *"and now the rumor has spread the same way we advertise our cake."*
>
> He said that the company has tried to counter the rumor by putting the Warner-Lambert logo on boxes and also by writing letters to 1500 congregations in New England. He said that one church group had blacklisted Entenmann products because of the rumored Moonies connection.
>
> According to Walter Weglein, manager of consumer communications for Warner-Lambert, the rumor started in Nassau County, Long Island, where the bakery is headquartered, although no one knows the source. He said the story has been fueled by a spoof on the show *"Saturday Night Live"* and has surfaced as far west as Chicago.
>
> *"In New England now it seems to be worse than anywhere,"* says Weglein.
>
> Joy Irvine, director of public affairs for Unification Church headquarters in New York, said the church had been getting calls on the rumor and that *"there is no truth in it."*
>
> She felt that the negative attitudes towards the church represented *"the same kind of bigoted stereotypes that Catholics encountered when they came to Boston."*
>
> Asked if the rumor had hurt the church, she said, *"No way. Their food's great."*

The press conference resulted in extensive media coverage locally and nationally. The campaign was successful and the rumor was doused almost immediately. During this period there were also brief episodes of rumors about the Moonies owning other enterprises. The ones that came to my attention were Genessee Beer, Baskin & Robbins Ice Cream parlors, and—of course—Celestial Seasonings, but the Entenmann's conflagration was the most severe.

The Joy of Winning

Let us look at a scaled-down version of a conspiracy rumor that followed the identical format of the others. This case had a local restaurant business for a target, a relatively small religious cult involved in the allegation, and the residents of a modest-size community for the population. The Joy of Dining was a recently opened restaurant in Orleans, Massachusetts. According to Gayle Fee, a writer for the *Cape Cod Times*, it had a good reputation and was a successful business enterprise. In the nearby area of Rock Harbor was a religious group called the Community of Jesus, an intense, demanding cult of 250 members who engaged in communal living and were reputed to be wealthy and growing more so. The surrounding residents tended to regard the group with bewilderment, suspicion, and apprehension. Stories were circulated about the goings-on at their commune and there was much speculation as to their expanding business interests.[17]

In 1982 one of the items of speculation was the Joy of Dining restaurant. Rumor was that the owner, John Gibbons, had gone into partnership with the Rock Harbor commune:[18]

> *Police Chief Chester A. Landers, a life-long town resident, said he has heard the rumor "everywhere."*
>
> *"It's all over the place," he said, "I've heard it from some of my officers, at roll call, on the street, at social gatherings, even from the chief in the next town."*
>
> *David Young, a chef at a cross-town restaurant, said he's heard the story from food and beverage salesmen, customers, and "a number of other people in the restaurant business."*
>
> *And a Harwich woman said she heard it from a friend who picked up his telephone to make a call and overheard two phone company repairmen on the line discussing the report.*
>
> *"It's almost impossible to get to the bottom of these kinds of false stories," said Landers. "It's like chasing shadows."*
>
> *"I've heard that some people, when they heard the rumor, have said, 'Well, I'll never eat there again.'"*
>
> *So late last week Gibbons began running ads in local news-*

papers and on radio stations, explaining that he is and always has been the only owner of the restaurant.

"When I first heard the story I just laughed," he said. "But it got to the point where it keeps getting asked and, well, we're not laughing anymore."

A year later he said that since his rebuttal campaign he had had no more rumor trouble and that everything was "going on fine."[19]

Several Cases of Beer Hearsay

Not all contemporary conspiracy rumors have to do with spiritual matters. There are other groups who feel uneasy—for example, gun owners. During hunting season, in particular, many hunters gather in the evening at "watering-holes." From time to time someone will offer the opinion that Gus Busch is behind organized efforts to pass gun control legislation and will state, "That is why I never drink Budweiser or Michelob." In Colorado, the Coors Company is the target of a boycott as a result of a rumor about their support of gun control. The irony is that both of these companies' heads are outspoken gun toters.[20]

In the early 1970s, Anheuser-Busch ran full-page ads in outdoor magazines denying the rumor. The Coors Company fought the rumor by having news interviews, providing denial notices for retail stores, and by sponsoring local gun clubs' trap shoots and pro-hunting documentary films. W.H. Coors, Chairman and Chief Executive of the brewing concern, said, "It would be an outrageous disregard for my own personal safety to support gun control legislation. Ever since my brother was murdered 19 years ago in an abortive kidnap attempt, I have always had a gun close by for my own personal protection. I want the privilege to use it effectively if need be. My personal arsenal comprises two shotguns, an army rifle, and two handguns, and I am proficient in the use of them all."[21] If bullets could stop rumors, maybe these could be taken care of, but the allegations against Busch and Coors persist.

Around the third week of November 1983 calls started coming into the Detroit office of The Stroh Brewery Company regarding an allegation that "a dollar from the sale of every case of Stroh beer was being given to the Jesse Jackson presi-

dential campaign fund." The amount of money would sometimes vary, but the implication was the same—Stroh was back-
ing Jesse Jackson. The inquiries had an accusatory ring rather
than one of enthusiasm, and it was clear to people in Stroh corporate communications that the rumor was part of a move to
boycott the beer. In addition to individuals calling, wholesalers
were contacting brand managers at Stroh to ask that something
be done; they were being confronted by their customers and
were losing sales as a result.[22] Carol Vollmer of corporate communications put together a two-sentence reply to be given over
the telephone at Stroh switchboards to anyone calling to ask
about the rumor: "It is against the law for a corporation to support any presidential candidate. Stroh is not doing so." No
mention was made of Jesse Jackson or anyone else. The problem came to the attention of William Weatherston, Vice President of Corporate Affairs. He became disturbed enough to talk
about the rumor to other executive officers, including Peter
Stroh, Chairman of the Board. Together they decided to make
a strong, direct move. In cooperation with the public relations
firm of A.M. Franco, the Stroh people composed a newspaper
advertisement which: (1) stated the rumor that the Stroh
Brewery Company supports presidential candidates; (2)
denied the rumor; (3) explained that it was illegal for them to
contribute to a political campaign; (4) offered to pay $25,000 to
the first person who could identify the party who started the
rumor; (5) give the number of a Chicago detective agency to
call with any information or evidence; (6) said they were ready
to take legal action.

Since the rumors were concentrated in the Chicago area,
advertisements were placed in eight Illinois and Indiana newspapers, including the *Chicago Tribune* and a Black newspaper,
the *Chicago Defender.* The half-page advertisement that
appeared in the sports section of the Sunday *Chicago Tribune*
on December 11, 1983 can be seen in Exhibit 4-9.

After the appearance of the ads, the media picked up the
story and gave it fairly extensive coverage. As would be
expected, neither the detective agency nor anyone else was able
to track down the person who started the rumor. Someone did
call to ask whether, if she turned in her friend as the instigator,
they could "split the $25,000 reward!"[23]

Following the placement of the advertisements and the

STROH OFFERS $25,000 TO STOP RUMORS!

There are rumors in the Illinois and Indiana areas that The Stroh Brewery Company is making contributions to presidential candidates. These rumors are not true.
They are completely, totally false!

The Stroh Brewery Company **does not** contribute to any political candidates' campaigns. We cannot. It is against the law for us to do so. Even if it were legal, we would not. We are in the business of selling our products nationally to consumers of legal drinking age. Our customers represent all political parties. We would not, and never will, anger any of our customers by supporting any candidate for office at any level of government!

However, we **do** contribute to certain non-partisan programs such as the current Statue of Liberty renovation effort. We were one of the first major corporate contributors to this nation-wide civic endeavor.

We believe that the rumors claiming The Stroh Brewery Company helps finance presidential campaigns are out-and-out attempts to slander The Stroh Brewery Company.

We saw that we had no choice but to speak to you, the public, on this issue. We want you to know the facts. It's unfortunate that we have been put in this position, but we will not turn away from an issue that affects us as an American corporation and affects you as the American consumer.

We are ready to take **all** legal and judicial actions against the person or persons responsible for beginning this rumor. We will pay a **$25,000 reward** to the first person who identifies to us the person or persons who began this rumor, where such identification leads to successful legal action by The Stroh Brewery Company. If you have information, please contact the Investigative Research Agency, Inc., at: (312) 745-1111

The Stroh Brewery Company, America's third largest brewer, is a private company solely owned and operated by the Stroh family. The Stroh family began brewing beer in Germany in the 1700s. The Stroh Brewery Company has brewed beer in America since 1850 when Bernhard Stroh settled in Detroit. The Stroh Brewery Company has always been, and plans to remain, family owned.

THE STROH BREWERY COMPANY

Exhibit 4-9   (Source: *Chicago Tribune*, December 11, 1983)

accompanying media coverage, no more rumors were reported
to the Stroh office, the Jesse Jackson campaign staff, or the
Investigative Research Agency, Inc.

Where Do They Come From, and Who Are the Carriers?

"How do these things get started?" is one of the most frequent
questions posed to me about rumors. Generally the source is
unknown because the story is by nature anonymous, with all
the absence of verifiability and responsibility that that concept
entails. Some people in corporations who are assigned the solv-
ing of rumor problems believe that if they could just trace a
story back through the chain of rumor bearers to that little
chap in the basement who is typing them out, they could tell
him to stop and the problem would be solved. It is highly
unlikely, however, that one can find the single person starting a
rumor, anymore than one can find the originator of a folk song,
a legend, or a joke. Rumors evolve, rather, as part of a social
process combining elements in various ways. Often the themes
are revivals of ones that were used in the past. They fade out,
then reappear again. The Satan charges were attached to
McDonald's, Procter & Gamble, and rock groups. The Moonies
series also showed the interchangeability of parts—dying out
here, popping up there, and all being variations on a theme.

The conspiracy rumor has a somewhat distinct orientation as
a commercial rumor. The point of the message is focused on the
allegation, not on the target. The reason the story travels is
because it emphasizes how threatening, powerful, or far-reach-
ing a conspiracy might be—"that it includes even Corporation
X." The point of the message is not about Corporation *X* but
about the extent of the conspiracy; naming the company only
illustrates the point. It was mentioned earlier that a rumor, to
be interesting, must travel through carriers who feel that the
message has relevance. This type of rumor requires a relatively
specialized population, one that has a primary interest in the
conspiracy and not the product. (In fact, many versions of the
telling include praise for the product along with the announcement of the unfortunate bond between the conspiracy and the
producer.)

Characteristically the population is under stress because of
fear of the movement in question and often has a more general

source of stress. As we know, both specific fears and free-floating anxieties promote participation in a rumor process. However, in conspiracy rumors the *content* of the allegation is *fear-specific.* The participating population is fearful of Satanic groups, Moonies, anti-gun people or what have you, and that is why that particular rumor is circulating among that population. Whatever general anxieties these people have add to the probability of their participation. There is reason to believe that people preoccupied with a fear of a hidden conspiracy are also high in general anxiety. If we are to understand conspiracy rumors of the commercial type, however, we have to understand where these fears come from. Although the allegations may seem baseless, they all have reasons.

Background for the Satan Conspiracy

When I first heard the conspiracy rumor about McDonald's, I was intrigued with the allegation component. How in the world did people come up with the Church of Satan? The charge in the message may have seemed bizarre to some people, but for those passing it around it was a familiar preoccupation. Just as is true for some early Christian and Gnostic groups, an "adversary cosmology" is basic to some varieties of fundamentalist Christianity. Essentially they hold that there are two forces in the universe struggling for control; one is headed up by God and the other by the Devil. People can choose to ally themselves with one or the other. Those who join the latter are Satanists, and they are powerful and well organized.

The principle operating here is called the "social construction of reality," in which the people making up a social group, through interaction and communication, define for one another what is "real" and what "exists." In social psychology there is another related concept, "the definition of the situation," which means that if a situation is defined by people as real, it will be real in its consequences. A segment of the population believes in Satan. These people believe that he has human followers and that these followers are engaged in a variety of acts to take over the world. In recent years, this topic has become a matter of concern among certain groups of fundamentalist Christians.

Robert Balch,[24] at the University of Montana, has done

research on Satanism. In the Rockies, people have connected
Satanism with a series of frightening events including murders,
attacks and disappearances. Speculation about these demonic
doings has been going on since the early 1970s. Balch says:[25]

> *Many of Missoula's churches have tried to counter the growing*
> *interest in the occult. Several of them have shown sensational*
> *movies warning Christians about Satan's ever-tightening grip on*
> *the world. In one of these,* Satan on the Loose, *scenes of perverse*
> *Satan worshippers writhing hypnotically in demonic rites are*
> *followed by the stern warning that "Satanist rituals like this are*
> *being conducted in your community!"*

The Defector Phenomenon

I have listened to tape recordings of Doreen Irvine,[26] a former
witch talking about the "world of darkness" and the Satanic
movement. Also I have heard tapes of John Todd,[27] who
claimed to have been a former Grand Druid of a witchcraft
order. John Todd was based in Dayton, Ohio. Since the time
"he found Jesus," he gave talks about the extent of the takeover threat to the world from the witchcraft movement. (These
people remind me of the speakers who made their living during
the 1950s talking to political fundamentalists about commun-
ism. In both cases, the threat was made horrendous enough to
justify handsome speaker's fees!) Todd told thousands of
followers in the Ohio area tales about how he helped organize
witchcraft circles in the military service, and he stated that
"every military station has a coven." He described witchcraft
as an international movement headed by Baron de Rothschild
and numbering among its top figures C.S. Lewis, J.P. Tolkein,
Jimmy Carter, Senator George McGovern, and David Rocke-
feller. According to Todd, the son of Lucifer has a timetable for
taking over the world in the 1980s.

An interview with a young woman printed in an article on
rumor in *Advertising Age*[28] told how she claimed to be a former
member of a satanic cult before becoming a Christian:

> *The main point for this articulate, bright-eyed young woman and*
> *others of her belief is, "You work for either one or the other." Or,*
> *as she stressed later in the conversation, "There are two forces,*
> *that's it!" The forces, as she sees them, are God and Satan.*
> *The basis for this theme, according to a woman who operates*

a Christian bookstore in this southwestern town, lies in the belief that Jesus is coming back. Before this can happen, believers say, there will be a seven-year period of adversity, brought about by the Antichrist. In a melding of religious and secular philosophy, the doctrine is being communicated in this way: The Jews, because they did not accept Christ as the Messiah, will be deceived by Satan in the form of a person who will be heralded as the Messiah. This person eventually will become the leader of a unified world, and is referred to in some writings as "the World Dictator."

James Gilbert, the Minister of Youth at the Church of Christ in Kaufman, a town of 5,000 southeast of Dallas, says he is intrigued "and scared" by the subliminal messages hidden in some rock music. Especially appalled by the technique of "backward masking," the 28-year-old minister says:[29]

Masking is evident to the conscious mind when the records are played backward. Instead of the garble usually heard on a backwards version, words are plainly descernible. These messages cannot be heard with the conscious mind when the record is played normally, but the subconscious mind retains them.

When played backwards, one verse in Led Zeppelin's 'Stairway to Heaven' says, "I will sing because I live with Satan." A second part of the song played backwards says, "There's no escaping it, my sweet Satan. The one will be the sad one who makes me sad, whose power is Satan."

In the spring of 1983 the television program *Entertainment This Week* had a segment devoted to the controversy between fundamentalists and the rock group "Kiss" on this question of Satanism and devilish subliminal messages. Obviously there are plenty of reasons for Satan-themed rumors to emerge and circulate in certain populations.

Moon Themes and Others

The allegation involving the Unification Church was very similar to the Satanism series. It had to do with corporate connections of a group that was looked on as threatening to some populations in our society. The populations who regarded the Moonie conspiracy as being relevant appeared to be more localized geographically and more general as to ideological background than the Satan rumor population. The people who feared Satanism had been exposed to singular information source about the threat; they thus shared not only the fear of Satanism but also a commitment to the belief that a movement is out there although not directly visible.

The Unification Church, on the other hand, exists. It doesn't require any special spiritual experience to know that fact or to feel threatened by it. Why do people feel uneasy about the Unification Church? It is an "outgroup," a "they." People have a tendency to be distrustful of outsiders. Not only is it an out-group, but it is a relatively new and unfamiliar, exotic religion from the Far East. The general public does not know much about the religion except that its organization is powerful. It has a large membership and large financial holdings, and it stages mass weddings in which the participants wait a year before consummating the marriage. It is one thing to be an obscure religious outgroup, but a *powerful* religious outgroup is something else. There is additional apprehension because of the Moonies' reputed recruiting methods. The alleged kidnapping and brainwashing of young people causes concern among parents. These features in combination result in the Moonies being an object of fear and hostility. These feelings are especially heightened in locations where the Moonies' presence is apparent. Moonie rumors are usually found in areas where they have acquired property or commercial operations; then Moonie rumors are relevant to the surrounding population, who are upset about their presence. Their entrepreneurial activities disturbed people in Florida and on the Northeast coast, and the rumor justified the feeling of threat. A similar scene, in a small way, was played out on Cape Cod with the Community of Jesus. In both cases the unwelcome presence of a religious group was looked upon as nonconventional, powerful, and threatening. This perception on the part of the surrounding population generated fear and hostility. The rumors legiti-mated the fear and hostility (as expressed in the call for a boycott).

A large proportion of hunters make up a special-interest population concerned with gun legislation. If they do not fear having their guns confiscated, it is not the fault of the National Rifle Association and other "right to bear arms" organizations whose existence depends largely on fears regarding gun owner-ship and the "survival of this nation." Simply imagine this scene, repeated around the country during hunting season: A group of concerned gun-owning hunters, some disappointed because of no kills for that day but all with a beer in hand. In such an atmosphere it would not be difficult for a "gun-banning rumor" to emerge and prevail.

In late 1983 the U.S. economy and the world situation seemed to be less threatening to the population at large, and nation-wide rumors were less apparent. However, the economy was a source of stress in various locations around the country, such as working-class areas in and around Chicago. Some plants were still closed and others had suffered production cutbacks. Many of these pockets of recession were populated by white workers who had migrated from the South. These areas were the ones reported to have the concentration of Jackson-Stroh rumors according to R. Sue Smith of Stroh Corporate Communications.[30] In addition to anxieties brought on by the general economic conditions, they also had specific fears concerning black power as manifested by Chicagoan Reverend Jesse Jackson's operation PUSH. Reverend Jackson's efforts for some time had been focused on pressuring corporations such as Coca Cola to increase employment opportunities for blacks. He was now also moving for political power within the Democratic Party. The white migrant workers' distress over the employment situation, combined with their traditional feelings about blacks, produced a strong psychological force for the Jackson-Stroh rumor to emerge and spread in these neighborhoods.

Other Contributing Factors: McDonald's as Archenemy

An item that comes to my attention from time to time is the response of people to commercial logos. Sometimes these emblems can add to corporations' vulnerability as targets. Ever since the "mark of Cain," people have looked for signs that would identify the bad guys. There are several key characteristics common to the admonitions of John Todd and similar midwestern alarmists. One is that the offenders are huge corporations and another is that they usually can be identified by something in their logo. (McDonald's fits the criterion easily.) A flawed syllogism could go something like this: The Satan conspiracy includes some of the most powerful firms in the United States. McDonald's is a large firm. Therefore,

McDonald's is part of the conspiracy. Bad logic, you may say, but the world is full of bad logicians.

Todd and his counterparts put great stress on logos, trademarks, and product design. They interpreted them for their followers and encouraged them to look for revealing indicators of sinister involvements. In his talks, Todd gave illustrations of designs, pointing out those that were straight (like arrows), round (like the red circle in a petroleum company logo), curved lines (like S's and dollar signs), and crossed lines (as in Xs). He also stressed the importance of double signs like the double X in Exxon and the double S in Kiss.[31] Given all these criteria, of course, not many corporations could escape speculation as to what meaning might be hidden in their logo or trademark, since many designs contain straight lines, crossed lines, curved lines, and circles.

Attention could have been focused on McDonald's by the appearance of their owner on the *Phil Donahue Show*. As you remember, the message in the McDonald's rumor included an attributed source. Most frequently it was the *Phil Donahue Show*, with guest Ray Kroc saying that he gave 20 percent of his income to the Church of Satan. Of course, he did not say any such thing, but some people wondered whether something was said that sounded like that statement or whether it had been suggested subliminally or otherwise. It was possible to obtain written transcripts of Kroc's guest appearances on *Tom Snyder, The Today Show*, and the *Phil Donahue Show*, and I read them all. I was even able to obtain an hour-long video tape of the *Phil Donahue Show*, which I viewed twice.

The only vague connection I could make was Ray Kroc's habit of darting his tongue in and out, in adder-like fashion, while talking. Also, on the *Phil Donahue Show* he displayed a rather casual attitude toward his several marriages that might have typed him as being on the same side of the aisle as the Devil to some members of the audience. Admittedly these possibilities are stretching a point, but possibly put together with other small connections they might form a pattern. More likely his guest appearances merely singled out McDonald's at a strategic time as being a successful organization, with double arches in its logo, thus making it a likely target.

Moon over Miami

Although Procter & Gamble is a huge operation, it is obvious that they had particular trouble because of their trademark. Their rumor problems seem especially convoluted, but I would like to propose a scenario.

Their first experience as a target was a brief one in Florida at a time when the Unification Church was buying property there. The property purchases account for the relevance of the *allegation* for the local population. The "snow birds" may have contributed to the *target* portion. During late fall and early winter, retired and semi-retired couples from rural Minnesota, Iowa, and Illinois head south for Texas and Florida. When these "logo-sensitized" midwesterners met some moonie uneasiness" among Floridians, it was highly likely that someone would notice the Procter & Gamble moon face.

Let's take the snow bird connection one step further. Winter ends and the midwesterners take their sun tan lotion, citrus fruit, and the Moonie–Procter & Gamble rumor back to Minnesota. Now we have a Moonie charge and Procter & Gamble as a target. The Moonie threat is not very relevant to Minnesota populations at that time, however, so the rumor does not survive very long. But—there remains a concern about Satanism, and *that* allegation becomes attached to the existing target, Procter & Gamble, with its suggestive logo.

Double Jeopardy

As we have seen, a corporation may become a target because it is already the target of another allegation. Such convergence-divergence switching occurs frequently. Consider a hypothetical exchange: Mrs. Pious has just left a church meeting where she heard the allegation that Ajax Foods Stores is part of an international nudist movement. The accusers even went so far as to state that all the company's employees are naked under their uniforms! She meets her neighbor, Mr. Grunch, at the bus stop. The night before, Mr. Grunch heard that Zilch, a grocery chain, puts thawed Siberian mammoth meat in its ground beef.

> *Mrs. Pious: Have you heard the awful story about Ajax?*
> *Mr. Grunch: Do you mean the one about putting mammoth meat in their hamburgers? I thought that was Zilch.*

Mrs. Pious: No, I mean about being part of the international nudist movement. I didn't know that Ajax puts mammoth meat in their ground meat, too!
Mr. Grunch (sighing): Are you saying that Zilch is part of the international movement? Where is this all going to end?

We now have four possible versions of a story that could be launched by Mrs. Pious and Mr. Grunch, not to mention the five people who were also waiting for a bus and overheard the whole confusing dialogue.

Another example of rumor confusion and amplification is the Moonie/Satan Procter & Gamble rumor. The Procter & Gamble company did not consider the early Midwest version much of a problem. In the Pacific Northwest, however, they had an overlay of the old McDonald's rumor. Instead of vague connections between the company and Satan, there was now a specific message, that "the president of Procter & Gamble appeared on the *Phil Donahue Show* and said he gave 20 percent of his earnings to the Church of Satan." About the only difference between the two versions was that the McDonald's one named Roy Kroc while the Procter & Gamble one did not name John Smale, apparently because the latter is relatively unknown to the public and does not write books or make television appearances.

Random Target Shooting

In many instances the targets can be explained only as a chance selection among prominent corporations. The Moonie–Entenmann rumor was undoubtedly a connection between apprehension of the Moonie movement and the popularity of Entenmann's products. I am not making an endorsement, nor do I consider myself a qualified judge of bakery products, but every time I talked about this rumor in class, students from the east would volunteer that "Entenmann's is the best." It was common for the message to include not only the allegation and the target, but also the pronouncement that the rumor-bearer was no longer buying Entenmann's product even though it was "the best." Such an element of sacrifice adds to the sense of seriousness on the part of the teller. Like giving up something for Lent or making a New Year's resolution, a sacrifice has to be something worthwhile in order to be impressive.

This added emphasis of sacrifice does not always occur. It occurred frequently with McDonald's reports but not often with Procter & Gamble. In fact a large proportion of the public does not know what products the company distributes.[32]

The gun control rumor is another example of the interchangeability of targets, depending on the prominence of the beer corporation in the region.

Stroh had loomed rapidly into the public awareness prior to the time of the Jesse Jackson rumor. It had taken over quite a few breweries, especially in the Midwest, making it one of the top three beer corporations in the nation. Its accompanying media promotions made it an important and famous brand name. Stroh is headquartered in Detroit, a predominantly black city, which may have added to the appropriateness of the brewery as a Jesse Jackson rumor target.

Endnotes

1. Ingrassia, Lawrence, "Rumor in Minnesota Says 'Moonies' Run Procter & Gamble," *Wall Street Journal* (March 26, 1980), p. 35.
2. Werwein, Austin C., "Logo Rumors Haunt P & G," *Washington Post* (March 26, 1980), p. B1.
3. Gilbert, Cathy, Procter & Gamble Public Affairs Division, personal conversation (February 8, 1983).
4. Gilbert, *op. cit.*
5. Salmans, Sandra, "P & G Battles with Rumors," *New York Times* (July 22, 1982), Business Section, p. 1.
6. "The Devil and P & G," *New York Times* (March 13, 1983), p. 23.
7. "Ann Landers", *New Orleans Times–Picayune/States–Item* (October 24, 1984).
8. "Devil Rumor Haunts P & G", *Wall Street Journal* (October 25, 1984).
9. Freeman, Laurie, "Rumor Returns to Bedevil P & G", *Advertising Age* (October 22, 1984).
10. Personal conversation (October 25, 1984).
11. Solomon, Jolie B., "Procter & Gamble Fights New Rumors of Link to Satanism," *Wall Street Journal* (November 8, 1984).
12. Solomon, *op. cit.*
13. Solomon, *op. cit.*
14. Solomon, *op. cit.*
15. Information reported here is based on conversation and interviews with Entenmann officials connected with the rumor project. There was also extensive media coverage of this case.
16. Trauch, Susan, "Entenmann's: It's Not Funny Anymore," *Boston Globe* (Nov. 10, 1981), p. 50.

17. Fee, Gayle, "Community of Jesus, Church Builds Membership and Controversy," *Sunday Cape Cod Times* (Nov. 8, 1981), p. 1.
18. Fee, Gayle, "Rumors Take the Joy Out of Business," *Cape Cod Times* (Feb. 26, 1982), p. 1.
19. Gibbons, John, personal interview (Feb. 20, 1983).
20. Montgomery, Jim, "Did you know...?," *Wall Street Journal* (Feb. 6, 1979), p. 15.
21. Montgomery, *op. cit.*
22. Smith, R. Sue, Corporate Communications, the Stroh Brewery Company; personal communication (Dec. 1, 1983).
23. Stroh buys ads to put down rumored tie to Jesse Jackson, *Detroit Free Press* (Dec. 9, 1983).
24. Balch, Robert, "The Creation of Demons: The Social Reality of Witchcraft and Satanism in Western Montana," unpublished manuscript (1975).
25. Balch, *op. cit.*
26. Irvine, Doreen, an address transcribed on a privately distributed tape recording.
27. Todd, John, addresses transcribed on a privately distributed tape recording.
28. "Deep Beliefs Move Anti-Satan Groups," *Advertising Age* (August 9, 1982), p. 3.
29. Luman, Betty A., "Rock: Backward Road to Depravity," U.P.I., *New Orleans, Times-Picayune/States-Item Spotlight* (January 8, 1982), p. 3.
30. Smith, R. Sue, *op. cit.*
31. Todd, John, *op. cit.*
32. "P & G Rumor Blitz Looks Like a Bomb," *Advertising Age* (August 9, 1982).

Chapter Five

CONTEMPORARY COMMERCIAL RUMORS, PART II: CONTAMINATION REFRAINS

The contamination rumor is focused on the target rather than on the allegation. It is an attack on the product and producer rather than a diatribe and warning about any threatening forces mentioned in the charge. In the McDonald's case, the emphasis was on the untrustworthy nature of a big corporation like McDonald's rather than on any threat from an "underground worm movement." Contamination rumors can be particularly devastating because they are relevant to a much wider population. This particular form of relevance is what I call the "ugh factor," which can elicit attention from almost everyone. Also, the message does not necessarily have to be believed in order to have a negative effect: The imagery conjured up by the charge can be repulsive enough to cause one to modify purchasing decisions, whether one believes the rumor or not. The idea that there are worms in McDonald's hamburgers may seem ridiculous, but the very thought on some level of consciousness may cause one to decide to get a pizza instead.

Some Cases in Point

A New Product Starts Off with a Bang

Another vivid rumor of the schoolyard variety involved a

confection put out by General Foods called "Pop Rocks." Pop Rocks is a candy, primarily for children, made of tiny spheres containing a small amount of carbon dioxide that makes a popping sound as the spheres dissolve in the mouth or are crunched between the teeth. The sound and accompanying sensation made the product the most innovative candy on the market since the jawbreaker. Before the candy "opened" to the general public, its previews were getting rave notices. The *New York Times* wrote about the prospects of the product with sparkling enthusiasm:[1]

> *Pop Rocks, subtitled Crackling Candy and made by General Foods, are the hottest smuggle since Coors Beer. Demand is exceeding supply, especially since General Foods is not yet supplying New York. Therefore, some candy store owners, who are receiving the packets by means General Foods professes not to know, are inking out the suggested retail price of 20 cents and charging what the tiny traffic will bear.*
>
> *Introduced in test markets in the United States toward the end of 1975 after its course of research into carbonation, Pop Rocks have been a hit, according to a spokesman for General Foods.*
>
> *"Children apparently liked it, and it has done well with children at all ages," said Rhoda Kaufman, the spokesman. For children who are rumored to be reselling their envelopes of Pop Rocks at prices that add up to $200 a kilo, Miss Kaufman predicted the probability of "a great future." As for other rumors, such as the rumor that Pop Rocks will blow off your taste buds or that Pop Rocks are never going into general distribution, she issued a denial. "It lends itself to myth making," she said.*

And "lend itself to myth making" it did. The *New York Times* accounts carried portents of rumor activity, but no one anticipated the extent of the problem until it was put on sale in the Northeast. The rumor concerned the explosive nature of Pop Rocks. A typical schoolyard account would be, "Some kid across town ate three packages of Pop Rocks and drank a bottle of soda, and his stomach exploded." Sometimes the attending doctor is named and sometimes the school where the student lockers have been searched and the candy confiscated is specified. In some versions, Mikey, a television personality, is the victim.[2] Actually the rumor had preceded the introduction to the Northeastern market. It had very likely moved in from the West Coast to the Midwest in the spring of 1977.[3]

General Foods became aware of a rumor problem in the fall of 1978, when there was a sort of "play on words" story going around Northern Pennsylvania about Mikey, the two-year-old kid in the General Foods breakfast cereal TV ads. (He ate the cereal at the instigation of his two brothers who would say, "Mikey likes it!") The cereal in question was "Life," a General Foods product. The story in question was, "Have you heard that Mikey lost his life by eating Pop Rocks?" Perhaps it started as a joke or a pun, but enough people took it seriously to make a sizeable number of phone calls to General Foods headquarters in White Plains, New York, asking, "Is it true that Mikey, that darling little boy, is dead from eating Pop Rocks?"[4] "We were getting calls morning, noon, and night," said Trécie Fennell. "We sought to squelch the rumor by denying it over the phone and by calling school principals. We thought we had succeeded and that everything had quieted down."[5]

Meanwhile the rollout of the product in the Northeast and Midwest was successful. Sales were zooming until late 1978, when they dropped substantially. In the second week of 1979 the rumor was apparent again, only it wasn't just Mikey but other children who died, were maimed, or got sick because they ate Pop Rocks. Ms. Fennell was working full time trying to handle the rumor.[6]

It was decided to run a telephone survey of a random sample of children and adults in the Midwest and Northeast areas. The results confirmed suspicions that there was a rumor problem, that it was serious, and that it was in the Northeast. Sales had zoomed to 500 million packages a year,[7] but by early 1979 the sales had dropped. Company officials would not say just how much, but they used the word "substantial."[8]

In February 1979 General Foods decided to confront the rumor problem. William A. Mitchell, the originator of Pop Rocks, said, "You could go either way—either ignoring the rumors or conquering them. We choose to conquer them."[9]

Mr. Mitchell was sent on a speaking tour of the East to talk about the safety of the product. Testimonials from the Food and Drug Administration were cited in press releases (see Exhibit 5-1), and food chemists and technologists were made available for interviews. An estimated $500,000 was spent on a full-page letter directed at parents in 45 major newspapers (see Exhibit 5-2).

Another letter went to customers (retail outlets), telling them about the product and the rumor, and advising them how to

FDA

TALK PAPER

FOOD AND DRUG ADMINISTRATION
U.S. Department of Health, Education, and Welfare
Public Health Service 5600 Fishers Lane Rockville, Maryland 20857

FDA Talk Papers are prepared by the Office of Public Affairs to guide FDA personnel in responding with consistency and accuracy to questions from the public on subjects of current interest. Talk Papers are subject to change as more information becomes available. Talk Papers are not intended for general distribution outside FDA, but all information in them is public, and full texts are releasable upon request.

T79- 4
January 24, 1979

Emil Corwin
202-245-1144

POP ROCKS/COSMIC CANDY UPDATE

Food and Drug Administration is again receiving inquiries about the safety of two candy products that have been marketed for almost three years in a number of Western and Southern States and are now being introduced in the Central and Eastern portions of the country, plus Florida.

The products are Pop Rocks and Cosmic Candy, manufactured by General Foods Corporation. Both are made of sugar, lactose (milk sugar), corn syrup, artificial flavors and colors, and processed with carbon dioxide to provide a crackling sensation in the mouth. Pop Rocks is in granular form and Cosmic Candy (previously called Space Dust) is in powdered form and contains in addition coconut oil (to prevent caking) and citric acid (for tartness). The amount of carbon dioxide is about one tenth of the amount in a 12-ounce can of carbonated soda.

FDA continues to investigate reports of illness or injury associated with Pop Rocks and Cosmic Candy. In approximately 50 reports investigated since the products were introduced, FDA has not been able to confirm that the candy caused illness or injury under normal conditions of use.

###

Exhibit 5-1

handle it (see Exhibit 5-3). Yet another series of letters went to school principals (see Exhibit 5-4). It thus was a four-pronged attack. Ms. Fennell said that "after we took these steps, the rumor virtually died out completely." General Foods is no longer in the carbonated candy business, but that is a marketing decision unrelated to the rumor.

A more recent TV commercial child-as-victim rumor appeared in May 1984. People were upset because of "the disappearance" of a boy who performed break dancing in a Pepsi-Cola commercial that featured Michael Jackson. The story was

An open letter to parents about Cosmic Candy™

**INVENTOR OF COSMIC CANDY, WILLIAM A. MITCHELL,
RESEARCH SCIENTIST, GENERAL FOODS CORPORATION**

Dear Mom & Dad:

My name is Bill Mitchell; I am a retired scientist for the General Foods Corporation of White Plains, New York.

I am also an inventor. I have the distinction, if you want to call it that, of "inventing" the new Cosmic Candy Sizzling Candy that is creating such a sensation around the country.

I have brought a lot of fun into the world with Cosmic Candy, I guess; but I am writing this letter because I want to assure you that the product is a safe one. Safety is one of my real concerns. I have seven children of my own, and 14 grandchildren.

WILD RUMORS

You have probably heard a lot of wild rumors about Cosmic Candy. I can assure you that we have investigated, and there is nothing to worry about. It seems to be the nature of this "fun" product that it also attracts rumors. This has been true wherever the product has been sold.

I think that is because it has the image of an exciting and mysterious product that causes those funny little sensations when you put a tiny bit on your tongue. The expression on people's faces when they do this for the first time is fun to watch, as you know.

Cosmic Candy is a candy. Its ingredients are the usual ones and chosen from those approved by the U.S. Food and Drug Administration in Washington, D.C. The FDA has reviewed Cosmic Candy and found it "safe" and acceptable.

The carbonated fizz in the candy, that causes the funny tingling, is equal to less than one-tenth the amount in a can of soda pop.

INVENTED IN 1956

My seven kids grew up with Cosmic Candy. I invented it in 1956 and I would make a little bit of it every once in a while to have it around the house for birthday parties and other fun occasions. I became very popular around our neighborhood!

Our Company finally decided to introduce it on the market. We tried it first in Canada and we couldn't make enough of it. It was an instant hit with the kids up there.

SAFE AND FUN

You know, you hear a lot of people talk about how "serious" business is, that people who work for big corporations don't have very much "fun".

Well "Cosmic Candy" is a proof that this isn't so. This is a fun product and a lot of people have enjoyed the product. The company has sold more than 500 million packages! Can you believe that?

Anyway, I just wanted to say to you that this product is a safe and fun product. If you'd like to write me, just drop me a line to:

Bill Mitchell
Cosmic Candy Inventor
General Foods Corporation
White Plains, New York

Exhibit 5-2

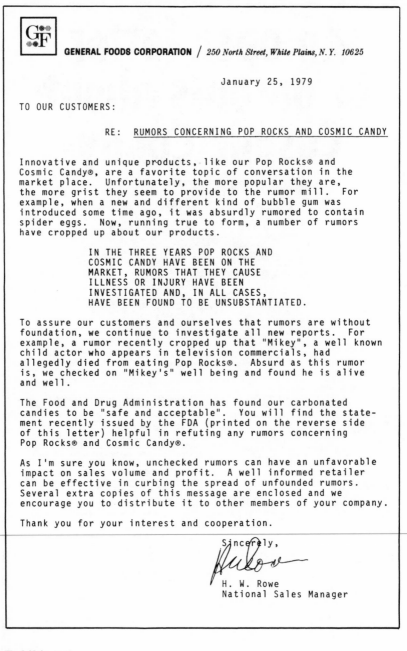

GENERAL FOODS CORPORATION / *250 North Street, White Plains, N.Y. 10625*

January 25, 1979

TO OUR CUSTOMERS:

RE: <u>RUMORS CONCERNING POP ROCKS AND COSMIC CANDY</u>

Innovative and unique products, like our Pop Rocks® and
Cosmic Candy®, are a favorite topic of conversation in the
market place. Unfortunately, the more popular they are,
the more grist they seem to provide to the rumor mill. For
example, when a new and different kind of bubble gum was
introduced some time ago, it was absurdly rumored to contain
spider eggs. Now, running true to form, a number of rumors
have cropped up about our products.

> IN THE THREE YEARS POP ROCKS AND
> COSMIC CANDY HAVE BEEN ON THE
> MARKET, RUMORS THAT THEY CAUSE
> ILLNESS OR INJURY HAVE BEEN
> INVESTIGATED AND, IN ALL CASES,
> HAVE BEEN FOUND TO BE UNSUBSTANTIATED.

To assure our customers and ourselves that rumors are without
foundation, we continue to investigate all new reports. For
example, a rumor recently cropped up that "Mikey", a well known
child actor who appears in television commercials, had
allegedly died from eating Pop Rocks®. Absurd as this rumor
is, we checked on "Mikey's" well being and found he is alive
and well.

The Food and Drug Administration has found our carbonated
candies to be "safe and acceptable". You will find the statement recently issued by the FDA (printed on the reverse side
of this letter) helpful in refuting any rumors concerning
Pop Rocks® and Cosmic Candy®.

As I'm sure you know, unchecked rumors can have an unfavorable
impact on sales volume and profit. A well informed retailer
can be effective in curbing the spread of unfounded rumors.
Several extra copies of this message are enclosed and we
encourage you to distribute it to other members of your company.

Thank you for your interest and cooperation.

Sincerely,

H. W. Rowe
National Sales Manager

Exhibit 5-3

GIF

GENERAL FOODS CORPORATION / *250 North Street, White Plains, N.Y. 10625*

April 12, 1979

Dear School Principal and Advisors:

In some areas, various false health and safety reports concerning two candy products manufactured by General Foods have been circulating among the public. We are writing to provide some reassuring information that we hope will be helpful to you should you receive questions from parents or pupils.

The products are carbonated candies, known as Pop Rocks and Cosmic Candy. They were developed in 1956 and were fully tested for safety before their introduction about three years ago. Each of the candies contains the same harmless carbonation contained in soda pop. All their ingredients are conventional and approved by the U.S. Food and Drug Administration which tested the candies and found them "safe and acceptable." Furthermore, marketing of the products in countries around the world has not produced a single authenticated health or safety problem. As a measure of their acceptability, more than 500 million packages of these carbonated candies have been sold here and abroad.

Pop Rocks and Cosmic Candy are fun candies and nothing more. Their sizzling effect comes from carbonation so mild that it is equal to less than a tenth of the amount in a can of soda pop.

Please be assured of the safety of these carbonated candies, and feel free to contact us if any questions arise that are not answered by this letter. You can reach a General Foods representative by calling this number: 914-683-2403.

Sincerely,

Gerald R. Saltzgaber

GRS:bao

NOTE TO PRINCIPAL: PLEASE ROUTE THIS LETTER AS DESIRED TO:

_____ Health Supervisor

_____ Home Economics Supervisor

_____ PTA President

Exhibit 5-4

that the boy, Alfonso Ribeiro, had had an accident while break dancing and had died from a broken neck. "I don't know where in the world the rumors are coming from" said Ken Ross, a spokesman for Pepsico, "there've been calls from all over the country".[10] A personal appearance on the *Phil Donahue Show* by Alfonso Ribeiro put an immediate end to the rumor.

Frightened Miss Muffet and Others

The "ugh" factor is particularly prevalent among children, and it appeals to the childishness that remains in all of us. Part of exploring the limitations and latitudes of norms while growing up is to indulge in what is currently known as "gross" stories and remarks. This behavior is especially common among boys, who tell stories so revolting and deviant that even to utter them bespeaks one's courage, audacity, and masculinity. Imagination and the ability to visualize serve as assets in telling such stories, which can easily become rumors. A good example of this form of allegation is the Bubble Yum rumor.

For many years, chewing gum for children was dominated by two bubble gum companies, Topps and Fleers. In 1976 Life Savers, a division of Squibb Corporation, put out a new type of bubble gum that was soft to begin with, so that the chewer would not have to get sore jaws working the material into a malleable texture.[11] The product was so successful that they had to cut back on advertising in order to keep up with the production demands of the retailers.

Then, in the New York metropolitan area, a rumor began to spread to the effect that Bubble Yum contained spider eggs—obviously a schoolyard "gross story."[12] The *Wall Street Journal* reported on March 24, 1977:[13]

Eleven-year-old Sean Wagner first heard the awful rumor three weeks ago in the locker room of the Y.M.C.A. in Ridgewood, N.Y. There were 10 or 15 kids all saying, "Don't eat it; it has spider eggs in it!" the fifth grader recalls. Now he thinks the story was false. But at the time it kept him from popping a piece of Bubble Yum into his mouth. He felt "kind of scared."

They quoted another interview: "Everyone says there's something weird about that gum," says nine-year-old Mark Doty of Brooklyn. "My friend told me there's spider eggs in it. I'm not sure that's true. It's a real chunky gum, so there might be something like that in it." Has he quit chewing it? "Yeah, I quit yesterday. I didn't get sick or anything, though. I'm chewing Trident now."[14]

The rumor spread as far as California. Sales did not seem adversly affected except in the New York area, but that was bad enough. After the story developed, the New York distributor had no more trouble supplying enough gum to retailers. The *Wall Street Journal* went on to describe the scene (March 24, 1977):[15]

> *Yet the rumor, especially in the New York area, is taking its toll. Nat Bernhard, owner of Carnel's in Port Washington, N.Y., says he used to sell 70 to 80 packs of Bubble Yum a day, but now sales have slipped "drastically."*
>
> *"One kid came in and said that she heard of a girl who fell asleep chewing it and woke up with spider webs on her face," Mr. Bernhard says. Another kid contradicted her and said that nine kids had died.*
>
> *And in Ridgewood [New Jersey] Mary Sharpe, owner with her husband of Sharpe's Stationery Store, said that Bubble Yum sales had plummeted there, too. "My husband heard the kids saying something was wrong with the gum, and he tried to check it out, but couldn't find any facts," she said. "We were selling 40 to 60 packs a day, and now we're lucky if we sell one or two."*

The Life Savers vice president of product management, Lawrence Hathaway, said that officials "agonized several weeks before deciding what to do" and that "the rumors we had to deal with were not large in overall sales, but in certain areas sales were affected. We were also concerned that the rumors were scaring the children."[16] In addition to hiring private investigators to try to track it down, the company spent an estimated $50,000–$100,000 on a publicity blitz. The campaign made news, from Walter Cronkite to the *Wall Street Journal.* Full-page ads in newspapers said, "Someone is telling very bad stories about a very good gum." This statement was followed with a detailed account of the care exercised in selecting ingredients and in packaging the product. Reprints of the advertisements and letters elaborating the message were sent to PTA organizations, school principals, and retailers in the affected areas. The rumors appeared to stop spreading, but for a long while sales in the New York area did not achieve the rates expected initially.[17]

President Mack Morris of Life Savers was quoted as saying a

few years later that his 1977 attack on "these malicious and absurd rumors about harmful ingredients or foreign materials in Bubble Yum kept the rumors from spreading but never completely restored consumer confidence around New York." Mr. Morris added:[18]

> ... *despite the ads and other anti-rumor efforts, including writing letters to school principals and PTA groups in the New York City area, we haven't achieved the success in New York we had expected; our per-capita sales here are below the rest of the country, even though the gum is a best-seller nationally.*
>
> *We really weren't able to pin down the rumor's origins, ... but the company's hiring of private investigators for that purpose produced a different benefit: It had the effect of saying, "Cut out the foolishness. This is serious."*

Eventually the effect of the rumor subsided, and as of this writing Bubble Yum, according to a marketing spokesperson, is the leading product in sales of soft bubble gum.[19]

A Brief for Sterility, and Chicken vs. Stork

There are other rumors, like the Jockey shorts rumor, that hang on for years but never attain a frightening degree of intensity. The rumor about Jockey shorts is that men who wear these shorts run the risk of being sterile because the snug-fitting garment increases scrotal temperature which in turn lowers sperm count. In 1979 William Herman, a vice president in charge of advertising and public relations, dismissed any problems resulting from the rumor by pointing out that use of the product had increased 10 percent over the decade. "Besides," he added, "I wear them and I have five kids."[20]

Despite that assurance, the association of the product with sterility persists. Dear Abby had an entire section on the topic (see Exhibit 5-5). John Berendt wrote an essay in the "Man at His Best" section of *Esquire Magazine.* He began, "Almost since the day the first pair was made fifty years ago, Jockey shorts have been at the heart of a smoldering controversy—one that breaks out in the open every so often. It has nothing to do with fashion." He went on to explain, "Jockey shorts were an instant success, but there were whispers that because they were tight, they could make a man sterile. The fact that lots of fathers have worn Jockey shorts never entirely quieted the

DEAR ABBY: A doctor told me that a couple of years ago he read some letters in your column stating that a man's fertility could be related to the kind of shorts he wore. This doctor also said this theory was scientifically valid. Will you please run those letters again?

—**Interested male**

DEAR INTERESTED: Glad to accommodate you. And how appropriate for Father's Day:

DEAR ABBY: I read with interest the letter from "Childless Couple," who were considering artificial insemination. This may help.

For four years my wife and I tried without success to have a child. We were both tested. She was fine, but the doctor said that because my sperm count was so low, my chances of fathering a child were slim. That's when we considered artificial insemination.

I saw a fertility specialist. He asked me what kind of shorts I wore. I told him I had worn jockey shorts for years. He suggested that I switch to boxer shorts — the loose-fitting kind, instead of the snugly fitting jockey type. When he explained why, I thought he was crazy, but I took his suggestion, and four months later my wife conceived! Our baby is due in March. I'm signing my real name, but please don't use it. Just sign me ...

— **Future Father**

DEAR FUTURE: When I read your letter, I laughed and threw it into my wastebasket. But I quit laughing (and quickly retrieved your letter) after reading several more bearing the same incredible message!

Read on for a short story that may help some for whom pregnancy is inconceivable:

DEAR ABBY: I am glad you printed that letter about jockey shorts. My husband and I had already started adoption proceedings when a neighbor, bless her heart, told me about the big difference my husband's shorts could make. We laughed at first, but two months after he started wearing loose boxer shorts, I got pregnant. We couldn't believe it.

We have three beautiful children now, and our family is completed, so my husband went back to wearing jockey shorts.

Thanks for educating the public, Abby. You can reach more people in one day than we could in a lifetime.

— **Pat in Houston**

DEAR PAT: And to make the theory of jockey shorts more binding, try this on for size:

DEAR ABBY: I recently read an article in a medical journal stating that if men continue to wear jockey shorts and tight jeans, the need for artificial insemination will increase drastically!

It stated: "The male anatomy was created so that the testicles draw close to the body in cold weather and drop in hot weather. It is a natural thermostat at work. Interference with this causes a serious drop in sperm count."

The article indicated that American men have increasingly lower sperm counts, and the problem is compounded by the wearing of tight clothing.

For population control throughout the world, wouldn't it be a great idea to export tight jeans?

— **B. McG. in San Diego**

DEAR ABBY: May I comment on your men's underwear debate? We in our brief-type "Fruit-of-the-Looms" remain fruitless, while our brothers in their boxer shorts remain "heir-conditioned."

Robert W.

DEAR ROBERT: I wish I'd thought of that.

DEAR ABBY: The fact that too-tight jeans may cause male sterility is nothing new. I wrote this little jingle back in 1970:

"If your jeans are too tight in the crotch
"Your parental potential is bad.
"Better let out your seams just a notch
"If you hope to be somebody's dad!"

— **B.M.S.**

Exhibit 5-5 (Source: The *Toronto Sunday Sun,* June 19, 1983, p. G-20)

rumors. For years the United States Army issued only boxer shorts, and today Army officials claim not to know why."[21] In a recent interview Mr. Herman said that the brief-type shorts are doing better than ever, representing the style of underwear preferred by 75 to 80 percent of American males. He says the rumor comes up in the media about every three years or so.[22]

Another sterility scare story had to do with Church's Fried Chicken. This time the problem was in the batter, which was alleged to contain chemical additives designed to render male consumers infertile. The rumor became conspicuous around January 1984 and circulated through the urban black section of southern California. The accusation was not new; it had popped up briefly in New Jersey two years earlier, but did not cause much of a problem.

The way the rumor was handled was somewhat unique in that the immediate response to it was not from the Church's organization but from Jim Bates, a congressman from the affected area. When he heard that black members of his constituency were concerned about the contents of the batter used in Church's chicken, he had samples sent to the Food and Drug Administration for analysis. After using gas chromatography and mass spectrometry, the Food and Drug Administration's laboratory reported that the product did not contain any drug products of the nature suspected. On the 24th of January 1984, the Reverend George Stevens, a special assistant to Representative Jim Bates, held a press conference in San Diego. Two West Coast officials of Church's appeared with the Reverend Stevens when he cited the results of the laboratory reports and declared that fears about Church's Fried Chicken were unfounded. Following the press conference, the rumor simply ceased to exist.[23]

In addition to the political intervention, the Church's case had another curious twist. I have categorized commercial rumors as conspiracy or contamination types. Although the charge against Church's was essentially of the contamination variety, there was a conspiracy angle to it also: Some versions of the rumor claimed that the chemical additives causing sterility existed as part of a plot that was concocted by the Ku Klux Klan.[24]

Teflon Rumor Sticks

Du Pont has not been close to being brought to its knees by rumors, but its representatives have had to deal with a pesky one for over three decades. Their experience is rather unique in the rumor collection because the message is technical in nature and the rumor is passed among specialists such as physicians, chemists, and safety engineers.

Company officials report the story as follows: Sometime in the mid-1950s, a rumor arose about a machinist who had smoked a cigarette contaminated with a little Teflon fluoro-carbon resin and subsequently died. In its most extreme form, the rumor claimed that after the machinist took one puff, his lungs filled up with fluid and he died within five minutes. It is interesting that the vehicle by which this rumor spread was official safety bulletins issued by responsible industrial concerns and military installations. In no case did a bulletin state that the fatality had occurred in the company that was issuing the bulletin.

A Dr. Zapp of the affiliated Haskell Laboratory has studied the problem and written a report on what he calls "human frailty—man's readiness to accept and repeat rumor."[25] The Du Pont people respond every time the "warning about the lethal features of Teflon" appears in a magazine, journal, or newsletter. The publication then issues a retraction, but the "warning" always seems to spread faster and further than any retraction story.

Generations of Vipers

Another recurring contamination rumor is the snake-in-the pocket story, which usually attacks a national chain. A recent version concerned a customer shopping at a K mart store in suburban Detroit: A woman trying on a coat made in Taiwan stuck her hand in a pocket and was bitten by a snake. In some accounts, the bite was fatal; in others, it merely resulted in her arm being amputated; in still other versions, she was bitten just enough to be uncomfortable. Snake eggs supposedly got into the clothes before they were shipped from the Orient and, enroute they incubated and hatched.[26] The rumor was written up as a news story in the *Wall Street Journal*:

*Not long ago, the story goes, a woman shopper at a K mart
store tried on a coat. As she put an arm through a sleeve she felt a
pricking sting. Thinking nothing of it, she went home. Then her
arm began to swell, so badly that she had to be rushed to a hospital where her arm was amputated.*

*Just what happened? Practically everybody in Detroit can tell
you: Somehow, a poisonous Asian snake had laid eggs in a carton
of Taiwan-made coats; they hatched inside the coat the woman
tried on, and one of the baby snakes bit her.*

K mart's Troy, Michigan headquarters, north of Detroit,
received about 20 calls (mainly from newspeople) who actually
bothered to try to track the story down. Susan McKelvey, the
chain's publicity director, said she did not know how the story
started. "Nobody has produced a victim," she observed.
"Nobody has come forward and said, 'I was bitten by a
snake.'" Miss McKelvey called a herpetologist to learn if veno-
mous snakes live on Taiwan. They do, but she said she was told
it was highly unlikely one could survive the long trip to Detroit.

Tom McIntyre, a reporter for WWJ radio, spent a day digging through hospital and police records in search of a victim.
"I got to play detective," he said, "but I found no victim."[27]

The Detroit *Free Press* and Detroit radio station WWJ took
on the role of rumor control by investigating the case and
publishing the negative results. As a result the K mart Detroit
version died out in two months, although other versions pop up
from time to time.

(Aside: While a guest on a Boston television program in
1981, I was discussing rumors in general, using the "K mart
snake" as an example. A woman in the audience got up and
volunteered that she knew that the K mart account was not
true, but she said that she *did* know of an instance of snake in
the pocket that happened at Sears & Roebuck—because she
was there! I chose not to embarrass her by pursuing the
matter.)

Finger-Licken UGH!

A particularly offensive rumor circulated in the seventies about
the fast-food outlet Kentucky Fried Chicken. Gary Fine
collected 115 variations of the theme and wrote it up as urban
folklore.[28] They range from a full-fledged "legend" version,

with a plot line, to a minimal allegation-target statement. An extended example goes as follows:[29]

> *On their way to the movies, a boy and his date stopped at a fast-food stand to purchase a bucket of fried chicken. At the show, the girl complained that one of her pieces of chicken was rather rough and "rubbery." Toward the end of the film she became violently ill. The boyfriend was so concerned at her sudden and intense condition that he drove her to the nearest hospital. The examining physician said that she appeared to have been poisoned, and asked the young man if he knew of any possible cause. The boy raced out to the car and burrowed through the half-consumed bucket of chicken, where he discovered an odd-shaped piece, half-eaten. He broke off the batter and realized that it was the remains of a poisoned rat, fried along with the chicken. The girl, having received a fatal amount of strychnine from the rat's body, died.*

A shorter version had it this way:

> *A woman was sitting in her living room, watching television and eating Kentucky Fried Chicken. After a couple of bites, she noticed that it tasted funny. When she turned on the lights, she saw that she was eating a rat with extra-crispy coating on it.*[30]

There is little record of what effect this story had on sales, how the company responded to the story, or what was the efficacy of their policy, if any, regarding the allegation. A spokesperson from the public relations office of Kentucky Fried Chicken refused to talk to me other than to say that the incident "did not happen, it was a rumor" and that "a rumor is a rumor."[31]

The Coke Series—It's the Real Thing

In contrast to the firestorm kind of contamination rumors there are some relatively harmless ones that have been around so long that they are almost an American tradition. These are low-level but persistent rumors. One of the more frequent targets is an American tradition itself, Coca-Cola. The Coca-Cola rumors include such charges as "it has narcotic ingredients," "its corrosive nature is detrimental to false teeth and iron nails," "it has intoxicating effects when combined with aspirin," and "Tab, which is advertised as a diet cola with one calorie, has a high caloric content." To set the record straight, Coco-Cola does not contain cocaine or any other drug; false teeth will not dissolve if put in a glass of Coke overnight; and nails will corrode if left in Coca-Cola for a long period of time, but this reaction will also occur if they are left in water; dropping an aspirin in your date's Coke will not make her drunk; and Tab has only one calorie (and it's all sugar-free). Coca-Cola has developed standard responses that are mailed to people inquiring about these absurd rumors, and the company's managers show few signs of panic over the possible loss of corporate profits because of them.[32]

Man Overboard

A fairly persistent and bizarre low-level genre is the "man in the vat" rumor. In this story a worker is supposed to have fallen into a vat (always a huge one) used to make some product such as tomato juice, a seasoning sauce, or soft drink beverages. Naturally Coca-Cola figures prominently in this rumor. At the lunch break of a symposium offered by the Coca-Cola Company, the head of the corporation noticed that I was slated to speak on rumors and extemporaneously inserted into his speech a story about his company's rumor problems in Brazil, where it was reported that two people had fallen into a vat of Coca-Cola. Later I asked for details on this Coca-Cola version of the vat rumor. The manager of industry and consumer affairs for Coca-Cola dug for the story, but his findings referred to only *one* worker who fell in a vat of Coca-Cola, and that occurred in one of the company's Far East plants. So, even in the same company, there are two different versions of the vat story, and these are in different parts of the world. The company spokesman wrote that the rumor about a worker falling into a production vat and contaminating the product is at least 30 years old, and that it recurs periodically in the Far East.[33] The oriental variant is as follows:

> In July of 1981 this rumor surfaced again. Within two weeks, it was widespread in one of the most populated cities in the Orient. Youngsters, who really did not believe the story themselves, cited family and friends as the source of their information. A review of the popular press indicated that a newspaper supplement had mentioned an old rumor in the context of a current article around the time the "new" rumor started.
>
> Disregarding where or how the rumor started, within one

month it did have an effect on industry sales. Additionally, it was gaining increased momentum, as evidenced by a letter to the editor and an article entitled, "A Rumor We Can't Ignore," in the daily press. At this point the industry association decided that the rumor could no longer be ignored and that positive action was indicated.

A little over one month from the time the rumor surfaced, an official statement denying the rumor was issued by the industry association and picked up by the local radio news. Space was purchased by the association in several newspapers and one youth magazine to repeat the same denial statement. Finally, a very positive article in the popular press entitled, "Worker-in-Vat Rumor Shot Down," put the rumor to rest.

In this instance the low-level vat rumor became big enough to be dealt with in the media.

There are undoubtedly other contamination rumors, but we have covered the main forms that have circulated in recent years. The new electronic communication revolution will no doubt produce innovative and imaginative rumors suited to the space age: "Have you heard about the boy who played Pac Man for 15 hours and ...?"

Where Do They Come From?
—Accounting for Contamination Rumors

As was mentioned previously, the emphasis of the message in a contamination rumor is different from that in a conspiracy rumor. There is a different charge-target relationship, with the point of the story directed against the target. The rumor is about a shocking situation that reflects just how bad things can be in our times. An essential feature of the target is that it be a large and prominent company. As one writer put it, "Each story blames a large corporation as significantly the leading seller of that class of food products .... The frequency of attachment of an urban legend to the largest company or corporation is so common as to be considered a law of urban folklore."[34] The bigger the target, the more attention-getting the story and the more valid the point of the message. A general underlying theme of contamination rumors is the untrustworthiness and irresponsibility of huge operations and the sense of deterioration in our society.

As we said in Chapter 2, rumors fulfill certain psychological needs of the participants. The idea of contamination can support one's world view of alienation and serve as an act of aggression against big symbolic targets. It is not just bigness that makes certain corporations vulnerable as targets but also the sense of a depersonalized presence looming in the community. (Contamination rumors of the type we are discussing in this book have not emerged as a problem in Western Europe. Countries there have not felt the impact of fast-food franchises and discount chains, but they are on their way and I predict that rumors will follow shortly).

In the United States the contamination genre has concentrated in recent years on fast-food franchises and their operations because they are outsiders who move into a neighborhood. They are seen as intruders who represent alternative values and ways of doing things and as absentee merchants who have pushed out the neighborhood grocery. They have also impinged on the home kitchen and the nurturant role of the wife-mother. The traditional family dinner table scene is not completely compatible with that including a giant pizza, a bucket of fried chicken, or a sack of cheeseburgers and fries brought in from one of these establishments. Those who sense this incongruity may welcome hostile hearsay against the depersonalized intruder.

Who Are the Contamination Carriers?

The population participating in contamination rumors is less discrete and less structured than that in conspiracy rumors. The people are motivated by personal needs and rumors that are gratifying to their alienation, anxiety, hostility, and need for attention. They are not members of anti-worm organizations or campaigns; rather, they direct their feelings toward the target rather than the allegation. General themes of contamination rumors are the untrustworthiness of big operations and a sense of deterioration in our society. People who are alienated and distressed about the state of the world are often attracted to contamination rumors. Such rumors enable the frustrated to vent their aggression against the "big guys" and the anxious to justify their feelings of anxiety. Many times contamination rumors are so extreme that they qualify as diversion, and they thus are tempting also to loners who seek attention.

The Wriggly Crawly Themes

Explaining the manifest content of an allegation is an exercise in *post factor* suppositions (otherwise known as guesswork). Again, the resultant message is a fortuitous combination of sparks and tinder. Events and the features of a product can play a part in the content of the message, but I believe that some underlying themes and images catch on because of universally shared meaning associated with certain symbolic forms.

Jung[35] talks about this symbolism in his writings on visionary rumors. He points out that certain symbolic themes have recurred in rumors throughout history. All of us, with or without Jung's help, are aware of the persistent presence of certain symbols in folklore art, literature, and dreams. What I am referring to here is the psychoanalytical idea that universal themes and symbols persist in the collective human unconscious. I do not subscribe to any mystical or super-organic theories or inherent archetypes that are genetically transmitted through countless generations, but I do believe that certain symbols and certain themes represent shared human experience. Such fears, conflicts, and paradoxes provide the basis for the selection and survival of topics in many contamination rumors.

How They Wormed Their Way into Burgers

The worm series can be approached from several directions and at different levels. In the symbolism that we spoke of earlier, the work has a dual paradoxical, positive-negative representation. The worm represents both life and death: It is associated with death in that it moves into a corpse, but it also stands for a form of life in that it emerges from and thrives on the dead body. It represents regeneration; witness the folk legends that the parts of a worm that is cut in half will survive and grow separately.

Earlier I mentioned that one of the prerequisites for a rumor to survive is for it to be an attention-getter. In the case of contamination rumors, this requirement can be met if the allegation of the message is repulsive. Worms certainly are considered sufficiently repulsive in that respect by members of our culture. (Remember the childhood trick of startling one's peers by picking up a string of spaghetti by the thumb and forefinger and twisting it so that it moves and looks alive?) Combine that fact with the suggestive appearance of the product. If one reflects upon red spirals of freshly ground hamburger meat, it does not take a great leap of imagination to visualize a pile of red worms. In young boys' "gross" stories there tend to be references not just to worms but to "big juicy worms." The *Wall Street Journal* quoted a flawed syllogism of mine as follows: "*A*. Raw hamburger looks like red worms. *B*. Red worms are big and juicy. *C*. Wendy's burgers are advertised as 'hot and juicy.'"[36] The implied conclusion assumes worms in the hamburger.

Also, at about the time of the worm rumors, there were promotions in the media for worm farm franchises. One of the uses cited for worms was a source of protein for a starving world. I actually heard an interview on radio in which one of the enterprising worm franchisers recited his recipes for worm cooking. Further, an article in the November 1977 *Reader's Digest*, "Hercules of the Soil, The Earthworm," told about the environmental and ecological miracles wrought by the versatile wriggly creatures. According to the writer, the earthworm not only is good for the soil but is 75 percent pure protein in dry form and can be used as food for poultry, pet, or even human consumption. "Palatable, if a bit chewy," the author said, and added, "A recent baking contest sponsored by worm growers awarded $500 to an apple sauce surprise cake containing crunchy nuggets of chopped worms." The article described one worm farmer's procedures for rigging up boxes with manure, peat moss, and litter where worms were placed and fed mashed grain. These containers attract worm predators, the article continued, "including birds, moles, snakes, and toads, which regard the farm as a *virtual McDonald's*."[37] This article appeared less than a year before the worm Big Mac Attack.

Horror Stories in the Schoolyard

Bubble Yum and Pop Rocks differ from the other targets in that their clientele are children. In a way they were almost fated to be plagued by some kind of rumor problem because of their outstanding initial popularity. Both products were huge successes in the trial marketing and early sales ventures, a fact that made them conspicuous objects for the schoolyard savant, one of those who likes to "one-up" his peers by ridiculing people or things that are popular—for example, telling the gang that police actually do not solve every crime the way they do on TV and that certain characters are "queer." These popular confection products were new, which also made them vulnerable to "inside" tale-telling by such "wise guys."

The Bubble Yum rumor depended on having a contaminant that was sensational but also minute, so that one could imagine its presence even though it was not physically visible. The eggs of spiders met both requirements. Spiders are crawly "repulsive" creatures, and some have a poisonous bite. The spider is generally considered a female symbol, with all the mystical implications that attend femininity. It is also a paradox, simultaneously representing domesticity, because it weaves, and hunting, because its web is a deadly snare. Additionally, the Bubble Yum rumor included not only the spider symbol but also the image of an egg, a life symbol.

Pop Rocks was in trouble from the very beginning. The "popping" nature of the product was so unusual that people began asking questions. During the product's initiation, *Newsweek* ran a story headed, "Pop Rocks Go Boom, Boom, Boom."[38]

> *Candy bars have become showbiz in recent years, and kids are positively blasé about such confections as Atomic Fireballs, Fu Man Chews, and Gob Stoppers. But if the results of test marketing in the Pacific Northwest are any indication, General Foods has set off two kinds of sensation with something called "Pop Rocks", fruit-flavored pellets of carbonated sugar that detonate a series of mini-explosions in the mouth and fire a giddy salvo down the gullet. "It sounds like a storm in your mouth," grins 10-year-old Davie Oliver of Menlo Park, California. "If you swallow them fast, they crackle all the way down!"*
>
> *Pop Rocks are stirring storms far beyond David's palate. In Seattle, the Food and Drug Administration set up a Pop Rocks hot line with a message to allay parental fears that the crackling candy might cause choking. In reality, it seems harmless enough; as the pellets dissolve, tiny bubbles of pressurized carbon dioxide pop and fizzle, resonating ferociously in the inner ear. General Foods appears to be preparing to sell Pop Rocks nationwide, but*

bootleg Pop Rocks have been showing up as far away as
Louisiana, where a 15-cent packet sells for up to $1.

At first the stories portrayed the candy as generally harmful,
causing people to choke, but the drama of the big bang aspect,
not to mention the orgiastic symbolism of an explosion, was
inevitably part of the reason for the allegation.

Fertility and the "Kernel"

People often believe that there must be some truth in a rumor
for it to have arisen and to persist. Although folklorists and
rumorologists often look for a "kernel of truth" behind a given
story, generally the allegations are unfounded. For example,
the charge associated with Jockey shorts, previously discussed,
is still unfounded as far as I know, but it is based on scientific
findings that the temperature of the testicles has something
to do with fertility. The rumor cites the evolutionary process as
designing male animals—including men—with testicles that
hang away from the heat of the body. It then observes that
Jockey shorts hold the testicles close to the body and thereby
raise their temperature.

Food for the rumor may date back to Robinson and Rock's
statement that "there have been reports that even relatively
simple forms of insulating clothing may affect male fertility
and that supportive Jockey shorts and suspensories would be
associated with an artificial elevation of the intrascrotal temperature."[39] They did research on male subjects wearing a
specially insulated athletic supporter for a period of 6-11
weeks. They found that, in every case, a remarkable decline in
spermatogenesis, to a minimum of 14.1 percent of pretreatment
level, occurred at about the sixth week after the start of insulation.[40] Although there is as yet no proof that wearing Jockey
shorts has long-term effects on fertility, one can understand
how rumors begin in view of the kind of speculation and
research on scrotal temperature that dates back to the 1920s.

In another case, also previously discussed, the participants
of the Church's Fried Chicken hearsay were people living in
pockets of stress. The economy was still in a bad state for most of
the black population. Threats to masculinity, as manifested in
fears regarding castration, potency, and fertility have been
around as long as the male psyche. Blacks are particularly

vulnerable to these fears because employment discrimination practices have been interpreted as negative to their manhood. Also, being the target of hostility makes a group sensitive to the fact that there are elements in society that would prefer to have them removed. A passive move towards genocide could come through reducing the black birth rate. Professionals I know who work with birth control programs in black communities say that they frequently encounter suspicions of their motivations for wanting "to control births" among blacks. Church's was the target of the rumor because of its policy of setting up franchises in low-value property sections of urban areas, making them very visible to the blacks there. Most of its clientele and employees are black.

The Ku Klux Klan connection seems obvious because of the organization's historic posture in anti-black activities. Larry Varney of Grey Advertising Agency, which has the Church's public relations account, offered an additional possibility. He heard that a television news program had presented material about the Ku Klux Klan, in which someone alleged that religious groups support the Klan even to the extent that Klan meeting "are often fed by churchs." He thinks that *church's* (with a steeple) became transposed to *Church's* (with a food counter). He does not know what program it was, or even if it occurred at all. It may be a rumor about the rumor.[41]

A Matter of Motivation

The Teflon rumor is the toughest one of all to explain. My best guess is that it stems from general rumor motivation: Du Pont is one of the biggest corporations in the world, a prestigious target.

Teflon has industrial uses, but it is much more widely known for its use in kitchen utensils. Since the 1930s I have heard rumors about contamination features associated with pots and pans. Aluminum utensils have been accused of causing cancer and enamel pots of causing appendicitis. This tradition of alleging contamination may provide the basis for the allegations.

To further exacerbate matters, editors of newsletters and trade journals are always in need of items as fillers. Further, given the brevity of their deadlines, they do not always have time to check things out. These circumstances may explain their motivation for joining the participating population.

Snakes in the Grass

The K mart snake, the man in the vat, and the Kentucky Fried
rat rumors are somewhat different from other commercial
rumors in that they resemble a legend. No matter how
extended or brief their versions, each is a story of something
happening to a designated individual. Each is reported as a
single event, not an ongoing condition or policy as you have
with additives or conspiracies. The *effect* may be continuous in
the implications that it could happen again and that the producers are not trustworthy.

In the K mart rumor we have snakes in the pockets of
garments which are being tried on. A snake in a pocket has
sexual symbolism obvious enough not to require further comment. In addition, snakes rank among the top universal
symbols in art, religion and legend; they are both attractive and
repulsive, having no legs and crawling on the ground. Existing
at the surface of the ground, they represent a liaison between
the underworld and surface world. At one time, science was
looked upon as a sinister and questionable endeavor akin to
alchemy and witchcraft. The snake was an ancient sign of
science as well as of the healing arts, and it represents both in
the contemporary medical symbol of the caduceus. Serpents
also appear frequently in urban lore, popping out of the mouths
of merry-go-round horses, file drawers, and the like. The K
mart rumor is an elaboration of this theme, with the addition
that the snakes are oriental. K mart, like many other retail outlets, imports clothes manufactured in Taiwan, Hong Kong, and
Korea. The menace of competition from Far East industries
and technologies is nowhere stronger than in Detroit, where
people have a real, non-archtypical fear of the Datsun and the
Toyota.

Fried Rodent—No Colonel of Truth

The contamination rumor directed against the Kentucky Fried
Chicken operation featured a fried rat. In Western culture, the
rat stands for disease, treachery, and disgust. We refer to someone as a "rat" as an appellation of disdain. In his analysis of

this particular rumor, Gary Fine says that a rat appears in the charge because the rat is a "common symbol of urban decay."[42] As we mentioned, the fast-food franchises are often regarded as unwanted intruders in neighborhoods. Professor Fine observes that "the growth of fast-food chains represents a change of function to profit-making enterprises, away from home cooking and the community or church supper. By implication this change symbolizes the decline of the family, the church, and community organizations in their most basic function, that of nourishment. That is to say, nourishment is now provided by those who strive for economic gain rather than for personal satisfaction."[43] For some, this development is a form of urban decay in its own right.

Having foreign elements in commercial food products is a very common item of hearsay. The core legend has been described in an article called "Foreign Matter in Food." It consists of the following:[44]

1. Someone purchases packaged or canned food, or goes to a restaurant.
2. Usually after the food has been eaten (but sometimes before), something horrifying and disgusting is found to have been in it.
3. The foreign matter is some part of a human being (or, in two variants, a whole body) or an animal.
4. Evidence is presented for or against the credibility of the incident.

The above was derived from accounts collected by the author Susan Domowitz and reproduced in an article. An example similar to the Kentucky Fried Chicken rumor is the one in which the teller describes what she heard from a friend about her visit to Aunt Jane's Pickle Company. The pickles are stored in large open vats and are unprotected. The friend reported seeing a number of large rats floating around in the vats with the pickles.[45]

In another variation, the owner of a cider mill near Okemos, Michigan, found two dead cats "in the bottom of a barrell [sic] of cider" which he had been selling. He did not know they were there until the cider got low enough in the barrel for him to see them. Apparently the cats "never effected [sic] the cider" because the owner never got any complaints about any of the cider. The bearer of this rumor heard the story from her uncle, who had a friend working at the mill.[46]

The Big Splash

The "man in the vat" is probably the most durable image involved in corporate rumors. The same image appears in literature—for example, in *Moby Dick* and *The Jungle*. Our earliest infant fear is that of falling, which is also often a dream subject and the culmination of many nightmares. The "man in the vat" rumor involving someone falling into a vat of liquid is a life-death apposition. No such rumor ever includes any mention of the body being taken out of the vat, leaving one with all the implications associated with ritual cannibalism and the recycling of life.

Part of Ms. Domowitz's article on "Foreign Matter in Food" tells of stories that derive their sensationalism from a human body, in part or whole, being the contaminant. A typical "part" version is as follows:[47] A group of women went into one of the restaurants in Flint that specialize in Italian food. While eating her spaghetti, one of them bit into something she was unable to chew, so she spit it into a Kleenex and put it into her pocket. The next day she sent her clothes to the cleaners without emptying the pockets, and in a short time she was visited by the police. After a brief investigation, the finger was traced to a place in Detroit that pre-cooked the spaghetti, and thence to the worker who had lost it.

The "whole" version is much more akin to the "man in the vat" story. One goes as follows:[48] At Aunt Jane's Pickle Company in Michigan, the pickles are sliced and put in a huge vat before being canned. One day when the packers reached the bottom of a barrel, they found one of the Mexican [sic] field workers ... all sliced up. Although the officials of the company tried to hush the story up, it did leak out.

And another one:[49] When goods arrive at XYZ warehouse in boxcars, the men who unload usually take a few samples home. One day a group of barrels labeled "alcohol" came in, and the men had a field day: They tapped a keg and drank until they could hold no more. Finally they decided that they had better get back to work and finish unloading the barrels. Being in a rather clumsy state, one of the men knocked over

the barrel they had tapped and split it open. There, preserved
in the alcohol they had been drinking, was a body!

K mart Is the Snatching Place

K mart figured largely but not exclusively in another series of
rumors that traveled around the country. The basic story concerned a woman who was with her little girl in a K mart located
in a suburban shopping center. When the woman noticed that
the little girl had disappeared, she frantically spoke to the
manager, who immediately locked all of the doors and conducted a systematic search of the premises. The little girl was
found in the ladies' rest room with a woman who had cut off her
hair and dressed her as a boy. There is no motivation ascribed
to the kidnapping, no real point to the story except that shopping centers are not safe places and one should be careful with
one's children there.

A version circulated through Texas and southern Louisiana
(both areas were going through bad economic times because of
problems in the oil industry). The following is a news item from
a New Orleans paper:[50]

> An unfounded rumor about a child kidnapping that never took
> place has left officials at the K mart department store in Chal-
> mette frustrated over what to do about it.
>
> According to the rumor, which has been sweeping St. Bernard
> Parish for more than a month, a woman supposedly tried to kid-
> nap a baby girl from the store by taking her into a restroom, cut-
> ting the child's hair, and dressing her to look like a boy. But, the
> rumor goes, the woman was arrested while trying to sneak the
> child out.
>
> But the St. Bernard Sheriff's Office said nothing like that has
> happened in the parish. "This is all just rumor," said Sheriff's
> Office information officer Peggy Poche. "We have heard the
> rumor from several people, but there is nothing to it. There's
> nothing that has been filed with this department and no arrests
> have been made."
>
> Poche said sheriff's deputies have reported being questioned
> about the rumor by their friends. "We don't know where it is coming
> from," Poche said.
>
> Officials at K mart don't think it is very funny. "It's a bad
> rumor that has gotten out of hand," a store official said. "There is
> no truth to any of it."
>
> "When we became aware of the rumors, we investigated," the
> K mart spokesman said, "but we couldn't find out anything.

*Every time an employee would say they had heard the rumor
again, we would try to trace it back and it would always be the
same thing—everybody had just heard it from someone else, but
no one had any information."*

Similar rumors have cropped up in other parishes from time to
time during the past year. Residents of eastern New Orleans and
St. Charles Parish have reported hearing stories about baby girls
whose hair was cut by adults trying to kidnap them from grocery
stores. But no record has been found of any kidnapping attempt
fitting those descriptions in recent years.

In Massachusetts the frequency of the reports prompted a
news piece in the *Boston Globe*:[51]

*If someone tells you the following story, don't believe it. It is
not true. It's a rumor circulating the country. It has been heard,
believed, and repeated around New England for almost a year. Its
persistence reflects a growing awareness and concern about children who disappear, some sociologists say, and plagues the heads of
stores in which the incident allegedly took place.*

According to the story, a child was missing in a suburban
department store in Foxborough, Danvers, Plymouth, Tewks-
bury, or perhaps some other community in which the story is
being told.

The rumor finally hit the big time when it made the Ann
Landers column.[52] It was the lead letter, with the following
heading: "Parents, Heed This Warning About Taking Kids in
Stores"

*Dear Ann Landers: Last week a woman was shopping in a
major chain store with her little girl. Her attention was diverted
for a minute, and she lost track of the child.*

When the frantic mother could not find the child anywhere in
the store, she notified a sales clerk, who called security. Security,
in accordance with store policy, immediately locked all the doors.
The police arrived within minutes. They could not find the child.
Finally, an employee located the little girl in the men's rest room.
The man who had taken her there had already given her a seda-
tive and was cutting off her hair in an attempt to camouflage her
appearance so he could carry her out unnoticed.

Three cheers for the clerk whose ingenuity cracked the case.
Three more for a store with a brave policy. And now a word to you
mothers out there: If you can't keep an eye or a hand on your
children when you go shopping, please leave them at home. An
awful lot of nuts are running loose these days.
                                                  —West Coast Warning
Dear West Coast: Your letter is a somber reminder of what can

happen if a child is allowed to wander off for even a moment. Thanks for the alert.

Ordinarily the Ann Landers column is where rumors go to die, but she was evidently taken in by this one.

Rest rooms by their nature are shielded from the public, and they have additional hidden compartments inside. They have been a locus for sinister doings in various tales. For some time there have been general reports of rest rooms being locations for drugging young ladies and whisking them away to prostitution rings. The addition of the "sedation" aspect in the Ann Landers version is an elaboration derived from the more traditional "drugged victims" stories.

Dirty Tricks

An invariable question on the subject of corporate rumors is, "Do you think such rumors are started by a rival company?" Although I am under no illusions about the ethical conduct of the participants in our free enterprise system, my answer is, "Probably not." It is more difficult to "start" a rumor by composing it and planting it somewhere than most people realize. The components of a message have to be particularly appropriate to the psychological receptivity of the population involved in a particular time and particular place. Accordingly it is more realistic to think of rumors as emerging and evolving than as being "started." Evolution, rather than creation, is the process by which both organisms and rumors survive. Another problem in "starting" rumors is that once they get started, they have a life of their own, and there is no telling how the story will develop. For instance, a conniving promoter of Astral Candy Company might manage to launch the rumor that Valley Candy Bars, a rival firm, has radioactive peanuts. Such a charge, however, can easily move from one target to another (convergent and divergent processes), and Astral Candy Company could be the one that ends up as the target of the rumor about using radioactive peanuts. The risk is much like that in using poison gas in warfare: The wind may change and blow all the gas back onto the initiating forces.

There has, however, been much speculation about dirty tricks and rumors. In fact, it is actually a rumor about rumors. In 1936 *Harper's Magazine* did an article called "Whispers for

Sale,"[53] which described how word-of-mouth communication was supposedly being sold as a form of advertising. The article told how some unnamed agencies hired actors to spread out throughout a city or a region and loudly extol the virtues of a product or a service. The actors would hold forth in buses, elevators, retail stores, and other such places. They would talk in a voice meant to be overheard and would say things such as, "I am a chauffeur, and I know a lot about automobiles and a lot about automobile tires. And I'm telling you that Firegood Tires are the best manufactured." And the other man would say, "Why do you say that?" And then the "chauffeur" would say, "Because they last longer, they give more mileage without trouble, and they are 100 percent blowout free." And then, supposedly, the story would be repeated by those who heard the stooges. The messages described in the article were all positive claims rather than the derogatory rumors we are used to today.

Robert LaPierre, a social psychologist at Stanford University at the time, wrote a book entitled, *Collective Behavior.* In it he said that attempts to plant stories about a product often result in confusion, with the names of products and corporations often switched. He believes that the practice, if it ever existed, was very quickly dropped.[54]

Of course individuals, on their own, can spread slander about anything they want to, and this applies to companies and products. Local distributors and salesmen have been known to capitalize on a rival product's current problem, referring to it when trying to sell their own product. In order to promote their own sales, they indulge in innuendo, say they heard something negative about the rival product, or participate in rumors about competitors. Lawsuits by corporations from time to time are directed against these types of people.[55]

Endnotes

1. Van Gelder, Lawrence, "Bootleg Candy: Suggested Retail Price Bites Dust," *New York Times* (May 19, 1978).
2. Montgomery, Jim, "Did You Know ...?", *Wall Street Journal* (February 6, 1979), p. 1.
3. Fine, Gary, "Folklore Diffusion Through Interactive Social Networks," *New York Journal of Folklore*, vol. 5 (1979), p. 87-126.

4. Fennell, Trécie, Assistant Manager, Corporate Communications Department, General Foods Corporation, personal interview (June 8, 1983).
5. Fennell, Trécie, *op. cit.*
6. Fennell, Trécie, *op. cit.*
7. Fennell, Trécie, *op. cit.*
8. Unger, Harlow, "Psst! Heard About Pop Rocks?," *Canadian Business* (June 1979), p. 39.
9. "Mitchell Busily Defends His Pop Rocks Candy," *New York Times* (February 26, 1979), sect. D. p. 2.
10. Personal interview with Ken Ross (May 22, 1984).
11. "The Bubble Gum Flap," *Product Marketing* (May 1977), p. 14.
12. "The Bubble Gum Flap," *op. cit.*
13. Cooney, John E., "Bubble Gum Maker Wants to Know How Rumor Started," *Wall Street Journal* (March 24, 1977), p. 1.
14. Cooney, John E., *op. cit.*
15. Cooney, John E., *op. cit.*
16. "The Bubble Gum Flap," *op. cit.*
17. Unger, Harlow, *op. cit.*
18. Montgomery, Jim, *op. cit.*
19. Personal interview with Mel Grayson, Public Relations Department, Bubble Yum (August 9, 1983).
20. Montgomery, Jim, *op. cit.*
21. Berendt, John, "Briefs," *Esquire* vol. 102 (July 1984), pp. 40-42.
22. Personal interview with William Herman (August 2, 1984).
23. Personal interview with Larry Varney, Grey Advertising Agency (March 21, 1984).
24. Personal interview with Larry Varney, *op. cit.*
25. Zapp, John H., Jr., "The Anatomy of a Rumor," privately circulated manuscript by E.I. du Pont de Nemours & Company, Inc.
26. Stevens, Charles, "K mart Has a Little Trouble Killing those Phantom Snakes from Asia," *Wall Street Journal* (November 20, 1981).
27. Stevens, Charles, *op. cit.*
28. Fine, Gary Allen, "The Kentucky Fried Rat: Legends and Modern Society," *Journal of the Folklore Institute*, vol. 17 (1980), pp. 222-243.
29. Fine, Gary Allen, *op. cit.*, pp. 229-230.
30. Fine, Gary Allen, *op. cit.*, pp. 230.
31. Personal conversation with Claire Lumpkin, Public Relations Department of Kentucky Fried Chicken, (March 10, 1983).
32. Personal interview with Roger Nunley, Manager, Industry and Consumer Affairs, The Coca-Cola Company (September 17, 1981).
33. Personal correspondence from Roger Nunley, Manager, Industry and Consumer Affairs, the Coca-Cola Company (October 16, 1981).
34. Fine, Gary Allen, *op. cit.*, p. 228.
35. Jung, Carl G., "A Visionary Rumor," *Journal of Analytical Psychology*, vol. 4 (1959), pp. 5-19.
36. Montgomery, Jim, "Did You Know ...?", *op. cit.*
37. Farmer, Jean F., "Hercules of the Soil: The Earthworm," *Reader's Digest* (November 1977), pp. 83-86.

38. "Pop Rocks Go Boom, Boom, Boom," *Newsweek* (June 13, 1977), p. 78.
39. Robinson, Derek, and John Rock, "Intrascrotal Hyperthermia Induced by Scrotal Insulation: Effect on Spermatogenesis," *Obstetrics and Gynecology*, vol. 29 (1967), pp. 217-223.
40. Robinson, Derek, *op. cit.*
41. Personal Interview, Larry Varney, *op. cit.*
42. Fine, Gary Allen, "The Kentucky Fried Rat," *op. cit.*
43. Fine, Gary Allen, "The Kentucky Fried Rat," *op. cit.*, p. 237.
44. Domowitz, Susan, "Foreign Matter in Food: A Legend Type," *Indian Folklore*, vol. 12 (1979).
45. Domowitz, Susan, *op. cit.*, p. 86.
46. Domowitz, Susan, *op. cit.*, p. 89.
47. Domowitz, Susan, *op. cit.*, p. 93.
48. Domowitz, Susan, *op. cit.*
49. Domowitz, Susan, *op. cit.*
50. Cannizaro, Steve, "Kidnap Rumor Bugs Officials at K mart," *New Orleans Times-Picayune/States Item* (August 13, 1984).
51. Richard, Ray, "Rumors of Store Kidnappings Persist in N.E. Despite Denials," *The Boston Globe* (August 16, 1984).
52. *Houston Chronicle* (November 21, 1984).
53. Little, R., and J.J. McCarthy, "Whispers for Sale," *Harpers Magazine* (February 1936), pp. 364-372.
54. LaPierre, Robert, *Collective Behavior* (New York: McGraw-Hill, 1938), pp. 179-180.
55. "The Devil and P & G," *New York Times* (March 13, 1983), p. 23.

Chapter Six

RUMOR AND ORAL COMMUNICATION NETWORKS

Not all rumor is word of mouth—that is, interpersonal communication—but a large amount of it is, and oral communication in general has special characteristics relevant to rumors. The disposition of rumor participants, as well as interpersonal patterns of communication, are also factors in oral rumor transmission. Let us examine these topics as a preliminary to discussion of networks.

Generally, word-of-mouth communication has a strong impact and is convincing. An early study on interpersonal communication was done by researchers Lazarsfeld, Berelson, and Gaudet. In their book, *The Peoples Choice*,[1] they discussed the extent to which interpersonal communication is important in a political campaign. In a later work, *Personal Influence*,[2] it was demonstrated that interpersonal communication is more influential in getting housewives to change their marketing habits than media advertising communications.

The reasons for the efficacy of face-to-face communications have been summarized by Charles Wright.[3] First, personal contacts are more casual, apparently less purposive, and more difficult to avoid than mass communications. Many people are highly selective of mass communications, avoiding materials that go against their personal opinions or that hold no interest for them. But people are less likely to anticipate the content of a personal communication or to take steps to avoid it. Second, face-to-face communication permits greater flexibility in content. If the communicator meets resistance from his audience, he can change his line of argument to adjust to their reactions. Third, the direct personal relationships involved in face-to-face communication can enhance the rewards for accepting the message or argument and the punishment for not. Fourth, many people are more likely to trust the judgement and viewpoint of persons whom they know and respect than that of an impersonal mass communicator. Fifth, by personal contact the communicator can sometimes achieve his purpose without actually persuading the audience to accept his point of view.

The characteristics of person-to-person communication in general are relevant to hearsay when it is transmitted in this fashion. However, the nature of the rumor message is specialized in that it is sensational and off-beat and is subject to various responses by the recipient. In the rumor process, the orientation of the person involved may vary. H. Taylor Buckner[4] describes what he calls three "sets" a person may have. A "critical" set is one in which the hearer has the background and motivation to evaluate critically the claims of the message and to repeat or not repeat it on the basis of his informed decision. An "uncritical" set involves an individual who lacks critical ability and cannot and/or will not evaluate the message objectively and therefore simply passes it on in one version or another. The third condition, in which a person hears a message and passes it on because he is told to, is called a "transmission" set. The transmitter is neither critical nor uncritical, but neutral.

The set most often found with consumer rumors is the uncritical one. Buckner says that "certain circumstances or emotions hamper or dominate the possibility of exercising critical ability. ... if believing a rumor fills a need of the individual, he will be much less likely to reject the rumor." In a previous chapter we discussed those various "needs."

As mentioned previously, the pattern of communication into which a message falls as it is passed from one person to another may vary. Both the disposition of the participant and the pattern of communication can combine to affect the course traveled by a bit of information.

Telephone—A Wrong Number

Of all the structural models of communicating, the most universally known is the one developed by Allport and Postman, who attempted to enhance the scientific status of rumor research by doing a laboratory experiment, as follows:[5]

> *Out of a college class or forum audience, a group of people—usually six or seven—are selected (ordinarily volunteers being used). They are asked to leave the room. It is customary not to tell them that the experiment pertains to rumor, though if such suspicion exists no harm is done, for studies show that the distortions that occur are but slightly affected by such knowledge. They are told only that they must listen carefully to what they will hear when they return to the room and repeat what they have heard "as exactly as possible."*
>
> *When the subjects have left the room, a slide depicting some detailed situation is thrown on the screen and some member of the audience is assigned the task of describing it (while looking at it) to the first subject. He is requested to include approximately twenty details in his description.*
>
> *After the initial description of the picture a member of the group of subjects is called back into the room and is placed in a position where he cannot see the picture on the projection screen although everyone else in the room can see it. (If no alcove or other architectural feature of the room provides a shielded location near the door where the subjects enter, some movable screen should be placed in an appropriate position before the experiment commences.)*
>
> *The first subject listens to the "eyewitness" account given him by the selected member of the audience or by the experimenter.*
>
> *A second subject is called into the room, taking his position beside the first subject. Both are unable to see the screen. The first subject then repeats as accurately as he can what he has heard about the scene (still visible to the audience on the screen). The first subject then takes a seat where he can observe the balance of the experiment.*
>
> *A third subject then takes his position next to the second and listens to his report.*
>
> *The procedure continues in the same manner until the last subject has repeated the story he has heard, and taken his seat (usually amidst laughter) to compare his final version with the original on the screen.*

Such experiments have led to the conclusion that, as a message is passed along, it goes through the following processes: (1) *leveling*—the accounts grow shorter, are more concise, and are more easily grasped; (2) *sharpening*—the perception, retention, and reporting of a limited number of details show selection; and (3) *assimilation*—the modifying of reports becomes more coherent and more consistent with the presuppositions and interest of the subjects.[6] Sometimes these principles apply to rumors, sometimes they do not.

The variations on this approach have resulted in what is probably the most widespread popular, psychological demonstration in the world. We have all at one time or another participated in or witnessed a game called "telephone," where a camp counselor, school teacher, or psychology professor gives an innocuous passage to the first participant, who whispers it to the next participant, who in turn whispers it to the third—and so on down the line. Finally, the anchor person repeats aloud the last version of the message, after which the originator repeats the ungarbled original statement. The group then discovers the point of the exercise: Messages become distorted through transmission.

"Telephone" and its variants, however, are actually of limited value as a rumor experiment. Rumors involve many more people than this demonstration implies, and they do not necessarily travel in a chain sequence. Rumor participants are highly motivated in transmitting and listening to the message; there is no "static" misperception that goes along with whispering in the ear.

The "telephone" message content itself is usually nothing of any particular interest, and thus there is no intrinsic motivation to pass it accurately from one person to another. The only motivation is the "transmission set," which merely entails going along with the instruction given by the leader. In a typical "telephone" situation there is no attempt to modify, to shape, or to be flexible. There is no feedback; the recipient does not ask questions or re-request elaboration or any kind of clarification. There are minimal—if any—facial cues, body gestures, or paralinguistic cues that can be used to emphasize the content of the message or to ascertain the receptivity of the hearer. Nor is there a rewarding experience to be gained from sharing in the message. In addition to the fact that the "telephone" message is not interesting, it is not supportive of mutual values and does not inspire gratification for accepting and passing it on to someone else.

The structural nature of "telephone" should also be noted. It assumes a linear pattern in the communication of messages (see Exhibit 6-1). Not only is it linear but it is transitive, in that *A* says something to *B*, *B* says something to *C*, and so forth. ("Transitive" here refers to the property of being passed on successively from member to member in a single non-reversible direction.) Rumors, on the contrary, very seldom travel in a direct line, although they sometimes may be transitive. If they followed a chain structure, any person along the line who was not interested in the rumor, who did not believe it, or who was critical or resistant in any way would, as they say, "dead end" it immediately. The rumor would be stopped. The probability of someone along the line being of this frame of mind is very high. The survival capacity of rumors, then, would be quite limited if the linear model were appropriate in describing them.

Branching Model: Barking up the Wrong Tree

Rumors, in fact, persist even though they are passed along in the basic form of telling and hearing. They spread rapidly and widely because they diffuse not in a linear, chain fashion but in a branching pattern. Exhibit 6-2 is based on the premise that if a message is interesting enough, it will be passed on to two or more people. Each person in turn will tell it to two or more people, and the message will fan out. No single person, no matter how unmotivated or critical, will stop it, as would happen in the chain model. The branching model still entails the left-right transitive, hearer-teller-hearer sequence. By branching, however, it reaches many more people in a short period of time and spreads rapidly.

Messages following this communication pattern are very difficult to stop. They pass through collections of people as an aggregate, even though these people do not have the interpersonal relations necessary to form a social structure. And even if there is any structure, it is of little importance in this pattern of rumor. From what we know from past rumors that follow this branching model, it seems that they are usually very dramatic, sensational rumors that are of general interest to everybody. People in a rumor network are highly motivated, sensitized to receive and pass on this message. Circumstances of this type usually involve what I earlier termed "crisis situa-

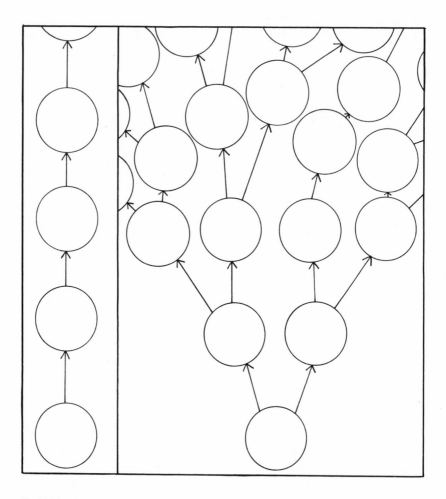

Exhibit 6-1   **Exhibit 6-2   Rumor (branching) communication.**
"Telephone"
(linear)
communication.

tions," where people are afraid or confused and eager to find out what is going on. In this state they welcome any sort of message that provides structure or meaning to events or that reinforces their heightened feelings. Such rumors can be generated during race riots, natural catastrophes, and wartime emergencies, and they can sweep through a population like a firestorm. An example is the explosion at Halifax, described by Shibutani as follows:[7]

During World War I, Halifax was the major Canadian terminal on the Atlantic, and by 1917 it had become the third largest port in the British Empire. For some time the possibility of the city's being shelled by Zeppelin raiders or by a German fleet had been discussed. All street lights had been darkened by military order, and the forts were fully manned.

Early in the morning of December 6, 1917, a French munitions ship loaded with trinitrotoluene reached Halifax from New York and was proceeding toward anchorage. Suddenly an empty Belgian relief ship swept in her way. There was a confusion of signals, a few maneuvers, and then the vessels collided. In Halifax 2,000 people were killed, 6,000 injured, 10,000 left homeless, and $35,000,000 of property was destroyed. One of the greatest single explosions of the prenuclear age left 300 acres in smoking waste.

It was one sudden, devastating blast; the earth shook, and homes crumbled. This was followed by a shower of debris, oil, shrapnel, glass, and wood. Water rushed forward from the sea in a gigantic tidal wave that swept past the pier and embankment into the lower streets. Nearly 200 were drowned. Trees were torn from the ground; poles were snapped; pedestrians were thrown violently into the air. Then came fire. The air was full of vapors which suddenly burst into flame. Soon there was nothing to the north but a roaring furnace.

At first all was in confusion. Some ran into their cellars; others ran into the street. Some ran to their shops, and those in shops ran home. Rescuers turned northward. Then came word, attributed to soldiers whose barracks were in the heart of the danger area, for everyone to flee southward to the open spaces. There was danger of another explosion! The alarm spread almost instantaneously. People needed no additional warning. They turned and fled. Hammers, shovels, and bandages were thrown aside. Stores were left wide open with piles of currency on their counters. Homes were vacated, and children were dragged along. Many never looked back. Some were scantily clad; women fled in their nightdresses, and a few were stark naked, their bodies blackened by soot and grime.

The refugees were dominated by one idea—the expected Germans. Eyes were turned upward, and many insisted they had seen a Zeppelin. A man from Dartmouth Heights, overlooking the harbor, claimed that he had heard a German shell shriek over him. Many contended that immediately after the explosion they saw a German fleet maneuvering at a distance. Few doubted that shells had actually come, and some warned others not to run because "two shots never fall in the same place." By evening, as refugees huddled together in theaters, churches, stables, box cars, and basements, the accepted explanation was a German assault.

As you can see from the above example, the only constraint

on the pattern of communication was the physical presence of the participants. Most rumors, however, do not follow this pattern. They are not all raging fires that go through everything in their path. Consumer rumors, as interpersonal communication, seldom follow this pattern. They are transmitted by interested parties who have an opportunity to talk with one another in some kind of existing social structure which provides a pathway for the communication. The importance of interpersonal affiliation, group membership, and group structure was pointed out by Paul Lazarsfeld when he studied the effect of mass media on the voting population in an election campaign.

Two-Step Flow

One of the early assumptions about mass media communication was that a transmission from a source would spread out indiscriminately through an aggregate of people. It was a type of water hose image in which the broadcaster or publisher would "spray out" information and anyone who was in the path would get wet. Lazarsfeld and his associates set up the study to see how "wet" the electorate would get.[8] The research design was one of the earlier panel studies done in survey research. (In a "panel study," the sample of people interviewed are periodically interviewed again to obtain an indication of change over time.) In this case, Lazarsfeld was studying the communication in an election campaign as it progressed, in order to see how it affected people's attitude and, ultimately, their voting behavior. In brief, he found that the campaign itself did very little to change people's orientations, candidate preference, or voting behavior, but he did come up with other findings. One was that people tend to select the aspects of a campaign that support their original positions. Thus, the information was used not for any kind of orientation, reorientation, or education but more for support of existing opinions.

Of even more interest to the purpose here was the finding that he could predict how a person was going to vote more by knowing the group the person belonged to than by evaluating his behavior regarding the campaign appeals. The consensus of the group to which the person belonged—not how many talks, speeches, or campaign messages the person listened to—seemed to dictate how one was going to vote and to form one's opinions about the election. In addition, Lazarsfeld found that in every group there was a person who seemed to be an opinion-leader. This person was more active in the campaign in terms of reading and listening and keeping informed. He was the one asked most often what he thought about the campaign as it progressed and was also the one who offered more of his own opinions *vis-à-vis* members. Such opinion-leaders were termed "influentials" in subsequent studies.

Lazarsfeld concluded from his research that the process of communication in an election campaign does not fit the model of a communication source spreading out and "spraying" a mass audience. Rather, a mass audience has a structure and communication progresses in what he called a "two-step flow": From the media source to the opinion-leader, and from the opinion-leader to the group. This model is certainly a simplified one, but it points out the importance of group membership and group structure in the communication process. Later studies confirmed this process of opinion-leaders and their influence, although it was subsequently discovered that there is not a single opinion-leader in a group but several, based on specialties. Thus, in a given group, there may be an opinion-leader in politics, another in marketing, and so forth. Nevertheless the structure of the group remains essentially that of the original model of the two-step flow, where the influentials pass information on to members of the group. The structure of group membership—who belongs to the group and who has prestige, power, and influence—will greatly influence how information is transmitted. A psychiatrist by the name of Moreno[9] published some findings that are compatible with the structural analysis of communication. In institutions for "delinquent girls" he used questionnaires to identify interpersonal preferences about who was attracted to whom as friends. He called these attraction patterns "sociometric diagrams" and the technique "sociometry." Sociometric analysis has since become an important technique in many types of social science research. Essentially, it asks people to indicate whom, for example, they would choose to work with on a task, whom they would prefer to do something with in a designated activity, or whom they would choose as a roommate. These choice patterns, as they are set up, indicate who belongs to what group or clique, who is the most popular, who seems to be the most attractive, and who is the most influential. It would seem reasonable to suppose that rumor transmission could very well be related to the membership and structure of such groups. In fact, in his book, *Who Shall Survive?*, Moreno discusses the relationship between interpersonal friendship patterns, the sociometric diagrams, and—among other things—the passage of rumors. He tells how the sociometric diagrams provide a description of the communication networks through which rumors and gossip passed in these training schools.

An example of a sociometric analysis applied specifically to the diffusion of rumor is the study reported by Gary Fine, who has done much research on folklore in general, and rumors, in particular. Fine reports a study in Southern Minnesota regarding the diffusion of rumor among pre-adolescents.[10] One of the rumors he studied in particular was the Pop Rocks rumor (referred to in Chapter Five). The story about Pop Rocks and the explosive quality of the product was circulated in the community Gary Fine was studying. He did an analysis of group membership structure with sociometric techniques and demonstrated how the Pop Rocks rumor was transmitted through groups such as school classes and athletic teams. A given story would circulate among members of a baseball team or a softball team, and sometimes among friends who attended the same school and were in the same grade.

One of the structural findings in Fine's research on Pop Rocks confirms an earlier observation that "isolates" (unpopular or least popular members of a group) often are the ones motivated to initiate the transmission of a sensational type of story such as rumors. In one sociometric network the rumor was first told by a member named Ronald. The sociometric choice patterns of this group showed that Ronald was a member that no one chose as a friend, making him an isolate. Similarly, in the transmission of the Satanism rumors, there seemed to be a tendency for the lower-status ministers to be the ones to initiate rumors within the religious network. These ministers in fundamentalist circles are classified as "weak brothers" as opposed to "strong brothers." They are not the ones who have charisma, not the ones who go out and proselytize and attract big crowds; they are usually sent to maintain and administer church organizations after the latter have been established.

Because rumor-passing is, among other things, an attention-getting device, isolates are more motivated to tell sensational stories just for the notoriety they confer. This situation is structurally opposite in direction from the two-step flow, in which high-prestige, influential opinion-leaders transmit information to the group. In this case, we start at the bottom and move up through the low-prestige ranks to the top. The process seems to be initiated by the isolate; then the story is transmitted by the opinion-leaders to the prestigious members of a group. In fact, when members of the clique were interviewed, they had forgotten—or simply did not acknowledge—Ronald, the part of the loner, in the Pop Rocks story. This pattern is an interesting twist on conventional network theory. In the traditional studies, the influentials have prestige and specialized "expertise" in certain areas of knowledge; in the case of rumors, the "influential" specializes in "contraband" non-verified information.

As we have said, messages such as rumors that are passed through interpersonal networks do not usually follow the linear pattern of "telephone" or even the branching pattern that we saw in Exhibit 6-2. Rather, rumors that are introduced into a group of interpersonal relations often exhibit the pattern of a network. Interpersonal networks involve multiple interactions in which the message is sent to several people in the group, is repeated and sent around again. As it is sent and received from several sources, various complicated patterns can result. A given individual can not only pass messages to more than one person but can also receive them from more than one person. Exhibit 6-3 illustrates rumor transmission of this network type.

H. Taylor Buckner has examined the nature of rumor transmission through what he calls "multiple interaction networks."[11] He indicated the combination of effects by taking into account disposition as well as structure. As mentioned earlier, he established several categories which he called sets. The "uncritical" set is the one into which most consumer rumors fall. The participant has very little information by which to evaluate the rumor as to its truth or falsity, but he passes it on to one or more individuals. He may speculate with the person with whom he is interacting as to the nature of the information, but he has very little of what is known as

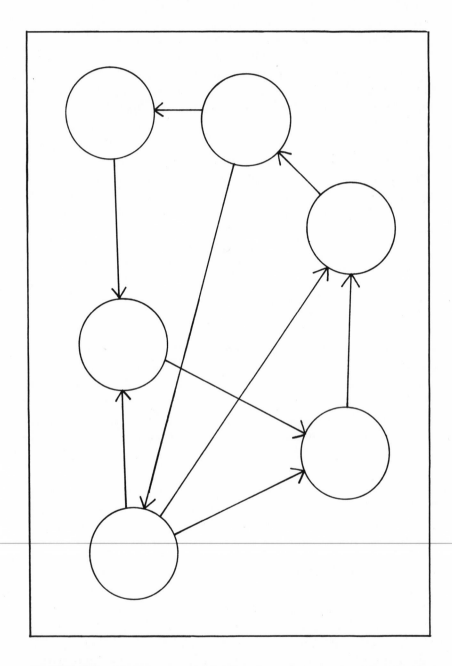

Exhibit 6-3   Rumor communication in an interpersonal network.

"objective" reality" testing. He may have reasons for wanting to accept the content of the rumor.

When product rumors and uncritical sets are involved with the multiple interaction network, the information being passed through has special qualities that will affect the nature of the message. As we have said repeatedly, a rumor must be passed on, must attract interest, and must be sensational and attention-getting in order to survive. A rumor is likely to be heard more than once in a network and to be passed on to the same person more than once. In such an instance, the possibility of the same message being augmented and exaggerated (to get additional attention) is increased: A participant not only tells the original story but modifies it to make it more sensational. The elaboration of the message serves the function of keeping the teller an active participant in the rumor process. Professor Buckner states, "The rumor will pick up new details in a dialectical process, synthesizing new rumors with new meanings, each of which may be modified to produce a better story or a better *Gestalt*. The more times the individual interacts, the greater will be the production of a false, distorted, and bizarre rumor, and in this situation the rumor will snowball."[12] The phenomenon is the reverse of Allport and Postman's leveling and sharpening, which may work when you have the rare occurrence of a chain pattern. In network transmissions that involve redundancy and repetition, however, one tends to be motivated toward elaboration of the story. If there is adding on and embellishing to provide interest, the result will be the opposite to leveling and sharpening. Individuals can, of course, belong to more than one network, which makes the process even more complicated.

Buckner did a secondary analysis of information diffusion in the state of Washington. An airplane was sent over a town to drop leaflets bearing slogans which were to be completed from information gathered from other members of the community. The reward was five pounds of coffee for anyone turning in the completed slogans to a designated address. The point of the study was to identify the information diffusion patterns in the community. Buckner also wanted to find out the parameters of the multiple interaction networks. He identified forty-two rumor networks, one of which is represented in Exhibit 6-4. As can be seen, many people belong to more than one network.

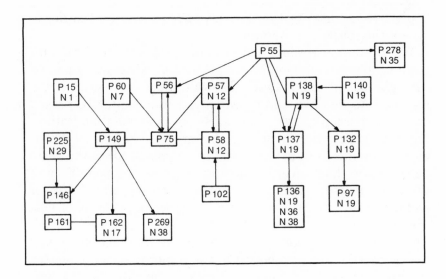

Exhibit 6-4   A communication network showing, among other things, the high communication frequency of isolates.

The *P* identifies the identification number of the person, *N* refers to the identification number of the network. The exhibit shows a phenomenon referred to earlier: Persons who do not belong to any network (isolates) tend to be the ones who have communicated the most often—that is, they seem to be the ones in most need of attention.

Even though we have emphasized the redundant non-transitive nature of the circuit network in most rumors, consumer rumor patterns can be more complicated. While the above model is appropriate for interpersonal communication *within* groups, message diffusion usually takes on a branching form when it travels between groups, from group to group (see Exhibit 6.4). Sometimes this diffusion from group to group occurs through mass media and sometimes through a combination of interpersonal networks and mass media.

Endnotes

1. Lazarsfeld, Paul, Bernard Berelson, and Hazel Gaudet, *The People's Choice* (New York: Columbia University Press, 1944).

2. Katz, Elihu, and Paul Lazarsfeld, *Personal Influence* (Glencoe, Ill.: The Free Press, 1955).

3. Wright, Charles, *Mass Communication* (New York: Random House, 1963).

4. Buckner, H. Taylor, "A Theory of Rumor Transmission," *Public Opinion Quarterly*, vol. 29 (1965), pp. 54-70.

5. Allport, Gordon, and Leo Postman, *The Psychology of Rumor* (New York: Henry Holt and Company, 1947).

6. Allport and Postman, *op. cit.*

7. Shibutani, Tomatsu, *Improvised News* (Indianapolis: Bobbs-Merrill Company, Inc., 1966), pp. 99-100.

8. Lazarsfeld, Berelson, and Gaudet, *op. cit.*

9. Moreno, Jakob L., *Who Shall Survive?* (Washington, D.C.: Nervous and Mental Disease Publishing Co., 1934).

10. Fine, Gary Allen, "Folklore Diffusion Through Interactive Social Networks," *New York Journal of Folklore*, vol. 5 (1979), pp. 87-126.

11. Buckner, *op. cit.*

12. Buckner, *op. cit.*

Chapter Seven

RUMOR AND MASS MEDIA

In order to understand fully the various types of rumor, we must look also into the influence of the mass media, both direct and indirect. In his classic treatise on rumors, *Improvised News*,[1] Tomatso Shibutani elaborates on Allport and Postman's[2] view that rumors can result from a combination of dramatic events and absence of news about these events. The type of rumors that result from failure by the media are usually related to what we call crisis or conflict situations: Rumors arise because people need or want information for making decisions, for adding structure to a situation, or just for providing some type of explanation for what is going on, but the news cannot be relied on either because there is *literally* a breakdown or because people *believe* there has been a breakdown. The first of these two kinds of failure is "objective"; the electronic or print media are simply unable to function because of some special event (for example, a disaster or civil strife). The second type is "subjective"; there may be a breakdown in the acquisition of news because the traditional sources are not allowed to produce news or are limited in the kind of news that they can produce (for example, censorship in a totalitarian state). For whatever reason, the public believes that it is not getting trustworthy accounts, and rumors fill the void.

In the marketplace, conspiracy rumors are sometimes associated with subjective media breakdown. These rumors involve suspected collusion and usually are associated with a feeling that powerful groups in business and industry are plotting against the best interests of the consumer and that the true story is being covered up by the media. For example, there are

rumors that "they" have the ability to manufacture automobiles that will run on water instead of gas; however, the big
oil interests are in collusion with the auto industry to maintain
the status quo and, of course, the media "play their part by
keeping the public from knowing about it." We have also heard
about the light bulb that never burns out and the razor blade
that never gets dull. During one of the recent oil crises, some
people thought that the shortage was contrived; in order to
justify and make sense out of their own frustration, these
people circulated rumors of large oil caches in the deserts of
Utah and Nevada and of whole fleets of oil tankers being held
outside the three-mile limit. Again, "they" were not letting the
public understand the true nature of the oil shortage, and there
was a general belief that the media were suppressing the facts.

My Friend the "Talking Head"

In some ways the media can find themselves playing a role in
rumors simply because of their success. In recent years, a
rather unique relationship has developed between rumors and
the media. For example, it is intriguing the way the message in
a rumor so often includes references to media sources—obviously an attempt to lend it credibility. What we have here is not
any failure of the media, in the eyes of the public or in the eyes
of the rumor transmitters, but its very success as a source of
information. There is no lack of public confidence in the media;
rather, they are looked upon as a reliable, authoritative
resource. Thus rumors containing allegations against products
and corporations are strengthened by references to alleged
presentations on programs such as the *Phil Donahue Show, 20/
20*, and *Sixty Minutes*; the rumor teller attempts to authenticate his story by attributing it to such a source. In the old days,
people used names of individuals whom they knew directly or
secondarily—for instance, one might say, "My brother has a
friend who works in City Hall, and he said such and such," or
"My neighbor's husband has a brother-in-law who works in the
police department, and he told me so and so." Today, programs
and public figures in the media are more likely to be used as the
references for authenticity.

It is not the media in general, however, but a special kind of
program or personality that is exploited to authenticate rumor

messages. Traditional, establishment-type media sources such as the *New York Times, Newsweek,* or regular TV news shows are not used. Rather, the unconventional, sensational programs that depend on investigative reporting, bizarre stories, or old-fashioned muckraking are in favor. Although it has not yet happened, it is not completely out of the question, for example, for the *Phil Donahue Show* to feature a big-time entrepreneur who belongs to the Church of Satan. Most of the media sources I have found involved in rumors are the kind that depend on shock and drama for their success.

Another point worth considering is the growing influence of media figures. A recent study showed that many people look upon certain media personalities as their friends—not just sources, but *friends.*[3] It may be that the extent to which some media enter into rumor messages is a function of this relationship. Today we live in a media society, where more and more of our information comes from, and more and more of our so-called relationships are with, "electronic personalities."[4] Because some people have little interaction with primary groups, they often relate to media personalities rather than to a friend or relative. Increased reliance on the media for information and identification of television communicators as friends and influentials very likely explain the new role media figures are playing as the credible source of rumor messages.

Media Networks

In Chapter 6 it was pointed out that rumors may generally be thought of as word-of-mouth, interpersonal communication, though not exclusively so. Unverified information can also be disseminated through successive media points and spread with great rapidity over vast distances. This phenomenon is similar to the spreading of jokes across the country by newspaper people. In the newspaper rooms years ago, people at the night desk wiled away the quiet hours sending jokes by telegraph and (later by teletype) across the country. This joke exchange is an example of media being a network of transmission.

Another example is the recycling of humor by college magazines. In any given publication, much of what is printed is picked up from other college humor magazines—trivia items, space-fillers, jokes, and other things of this nature. The result is an almost endless repetition of certain items. A former humor magazine editor did a study which showed that some old material was still being recycled in college humor magazines forty years later.[5] A very similar process can occur with rumors, when a story appearing in one publication is picked up by another or by other media. An editor may read an item in another paper and include it in his own column, which is read by a radio newscaster, whose broadcast is heard by a person in another city, who writes a letter to an editor, and so forth. The essential thing to keep in mind is that media can be strategic elements in rumor transmission and that the potential extent and rapidity of diffusion is awesome. The structure of such a network is usually a form of branching pattern (see Exhibit 4-2) discussed earlier. When non-media people receive the message, it then may become part of interpersonal communication, depending on the needs and interests of the persons involved.

There are, of course, varieties of media. The minor, unheard of media sources can play a major part in certain types of rumor proliferation. For example, company house organs, reports, newsletters, trade papers, and special interest publications come out by the thousand every month. They all need items to fill space. Many are low-budget, so they tend to borrow from other publications; and being one-person operations, they are without strong commitment to research or checking of facts. There are also amateur transmitters of information in the media, such as those who write letters or phone talk shows. Letters to the editor also can be a fairly important means of sending a message. People who are habitual letter writers usually have strong views; they need to make their point, and they are likely to seize upon hearsay and stories that support their position. One breed of letter-to-the-editor writers send dozens of the same letters to editors throughout the country, sometimes signed and sometimes not. If a rumor that fits their point of view gets plugged into one of these letters, the results can be widespread.

A good example of the type of rumor we are talking about is the one about the fatal consequences of getting Teflon material on a cigarette. Almost all the links in this rumor network were media points. The vehicle by which this rumor spread was usually official safety bulletins put out by factories, industry groups, and military installations. (In no case did any of the reports state that the fatality had occurred in the company or on the military base that was issuing the bulletin.) In the early days of the rumor, it was traced to an aircraft plant on the East Coast. The people there said they got the story from an eastern Air Force installation. One Air Force installation said they got it from an aircraft plant on the West Coast. Finally the U.S. Air Force issued a notice through the Inspector General saying that the rumor was false and unsubstantiated. However, it came back in about a year's time and started appearing again, usually in factory safety bulletins but also in Air Force installations. One company, for instance, not only copied the story from another company's bulletin but sent it to 137 different locations in the United States, Canada, and New Mexico. The source they quoted had long since retracted the rumor, but that fact was overlooked. Later the company sent out 137 copies disavowing and retracting the rumor, but of course by that time it had proliferated again.

Following the Pathways

An example of the pathways of rumor is given in an article by Robert Zapp.[6] He begins by pointing out a warning about the hazards of Teflon issued in the *Canadian Medical Association Journal* in the form of a letter to the editor from an industrial physician in British Columbia. It contained verbatim quotations from a safety bulletin issued by a chemical company in New York, whose author said that his information was derived from a publication of the British Columbia Fire Chiefs Association. Doctor Zapp thinks that the rumor reached Kitimat, British Columbia, by way of a U.S. Air Force publication in Texas. That publication was picked up by an Air Force medical officer in Michigan, who published the story in his base information bulletin. The fire chiefs of that base took a copy of the article to a convention of fire chiefs in Detroit. From there it went to the British Columbia Fire Chief's publication, where it was seen by a physician from Kitimat who put it in the letters column of the Canadian Medical Association Journal.

A very similar sequence occurred in the medical safety newsletter network. The story there deals with alleged hazards of wearing contact lenses in industrial settings. The following is the account as it appeared in the *New Orleans Times-Picayune States-Item:*[7]

A story about two men who were blinded when their contact lenses stuck to their corneas was circulated throughout New Orleans before the Coast Guard admitted it was false. The report was in the Coast Guard's Marine Safety Newsletter of May 18 [1983], which the New Orleans Steamship Association distributed to its members. According to the story, which the Coast Guard retracted last month, electrical sparks generated microwaves that dried up the fluid between the men's eyes and their contacts, thereby fusing the lenses to their eyeballs.

"Upon returning to their homes from work," the newsletter said, "they both removed their contact lenses and the cornea of each eye was removed along with the lenses. Result: permanent blindness."

"That's anatomically impossible," said Dr. Herbert E. Kaufman, director of the Louisiana State University Eye Center. Ultraviolet light from industrial sparks might cause minor damage to the surface of the cornea, but contacts should act as a shield to decrease the amount of ultraviolet light getting to the eye, said Dr. Peter Kastl, head of Tulane University Medical Center's contact lens section. "Well-fitted contact lenses, when properly cared for, should not cause any problem to people's eyes," said Kastl, an assistant professor of ophthalmology and biochemistry. "To dry up fluids (in the eye) as the story described would cause burns to the eye, and a burn like that would burn the rest of your face, too. Contact lenses would be the last worry you'd have."

Kaufman, Kastl, and other area eye doctors have been repeating these reassurances for the past two months to people who have read or heard about the report. Kastl also has gone on radio talk shows to scotch the story. Several ophthalmologists reported a handful of inquiries, but Dr. Rise Delmar Ochsner said there hasn't been a panic.

The steamship association, which circulates the newsletter to its nearly six dozen corporate members, has received no feedback on the article, said Septime Bossier, an association staff member. "But we only disseminate the Marine Safety Newsletter," he said, "so we wouldn't have any knowledge of it (the article) at all."

Lt. Cmdr. Richard E. Ford, chief of the Coast Guard's Port Safety Division, said the item was published because his office received complaints from welders about working conditions. Because the light is so intense, welding can be "like looking into the sun," he said.

Nancy Solomon, the spokeswoman for the American Academy of Ophthalmology, said the story is a distorted version of a 1967 incident in Baltimore. In that accident, a welder was working

> *near an electrical switch box when it exploded. Although he suf-*
> *fered corneal ulcers, his vision returned to normal in a few days,*
> *Solomon said.*
>
> *By the time the story reached New Orleans, it involved two*
> *Pittsburgh workers who were blinded. Spokesmen for the busi-*
> *nesses named in the story—Duquesne Electric Co. and United*
> *Parcel Service—said such incidents never happened.*

The story has also been disseminated in the United Auto Workers Union, the Civil Service Employees Association, the Maryland Department of Transportation, and the Baltimore Police Department, Solomon said.

After Ford's superiors told him the story was false, the newsletter published a correction last month, he said.

Price of Cabbages

An incredible case of rumor proliferation has been documented by Max Hall in an article entitled, "The Great Cabbage Hoax."[8] This story concerned the establishment of prices for cabbages in a marketplace where the customers were U.S. taxpayers. The author did an unusually detailed job of describing the spread of the hoax. (Note: rumors spread by media can be more easily documented than the person-to-person, word-of-mouth type of rumors.)

In the 1950s, Hall was the director of public information for a federal agency known as the Office of Price Stabilization (OPS). He became concerned with a rumor that dealt with OPS: "The Gettysburg Address contains 266 words; the Ten Commandments, 297; the Declaration of Independence, 300. And a recent directive from the Office of Price Stabilization written to regulate the price of cabbages contains many more than 300 words." In fact, OPS had never sent out any order or directive even vaguely connected with the price of cabbage.

As far as Hall was able to discover, the cabbage story appeared first in 1951 in a journal called the *New England Homestead*, a semi-monthly farm journal published in Springfield, Massachusetts. A month later it appeared in the *New York Daily News* (a circulation of 2,200,000), printed in the form of a letter to the editor. Two months later the cabbage hoax appeared in what is known as the *In-land Printer*, a monthly trade paper in Chicago; the editor used it in a column and credited the *New England Homestead*.

At the same time, the cabbage anecdote appeared in a mimeographed circular on the letterhead of Glaser-Crandell Company, a Chicago producer of pickles. The president of the pickle company said that he got the information from the news-letter of the Grocery Manufacturers of America. The president of the Grocery Manufacturers of America said that he got it at a meeting in 'New York where copies of this item were distri-buted. It showed up in many other places in letters to the editor, and it was featured in a column by Dr. George W. Crane called, "Test Your Horse Sense," in which the length of the Declaration of Independence was corrected to 1,348 words (which is more nearly accurate), but no check was run on the accuracy of the OPS order to control the price of cabbage. A businessman in Louisville put the story on printed blotters. The story was told by a vice president of Safeway Stores when he spoke to a rotary club in San Bernardino, and it was reported in the San Bernardino *Telegram.* The *Director's Digest of the United States Savings and Loan* published the story; they said they got it from the St. Paul *Pioneer Press.*

The *Wall Street Journal* shortly afterwards printed the story, where Morgan Beatty read it and repeated it on NBC radio that very same evening. On the NBC quiz program entitled "Double or Nothing," the master of ceremonies, Walter O'Keefe, incorporated it into a "Grand Slam" question. He announced that the contestant who came close to the correct answer would win eighty dollars. The question was something like, "Lincoln's Gettysburg Address contains 266 words; the Ten Commandments contain 297; the Declaration of In-dependence contains 300 words. How many words are in the OPS order to reduce the price of cabbage?" He subsequently proclaimed the correct answer was 26,911. The OPS informa-tion officer in Los Angeles contacted the program director and asked that a correction be made. Walter O'Keefe reported that the sponsor, the Campbell Soup Company, did not want any correction made. The OPS man then wrote to the advertising agency in charge of the program for Campbell Soup, and asked for a retraction. Their answer was that they found it bad busi-ness to publicize such mistakes in a quiz program. The cabbages rolled on.

The *Washington Times Herald* published a letter from a Harrisburg, Virginia man who began this letter, "It is the consensus of most people in the rural areas and communities of this nation that this Administration is in more ways corrupt than any that has ever held sway in our capital." He then went on to prove this point by telling the cabbage story. He said he got the story from the Rotary Club's weekly *Rotorgraph.* The rumor was printed in Walter Winchell's column, also in Bennett Cerf's Column called "*Tradewinds*" in the *Saturday Review.* It was in a column titled "Flotsom and Jetsom" in an issue of *Tide Magazine,* a magazine for the advertising profession, who said they got it from the *Sales Executive Club* of Pittsburgh, which is the same organization whose newsletter Winchell used for his version of the cabbage story. It showed up in the Dallas *Times-Herald* under what they call "Today's Chuckle."

The next year the cabbage story appeared in the *Saturday Evening Post* on the editorial page. It was compared to official Soviet pronouncements and used to show how the Soviets were even more bumble-headed than the "socialist-minded Washingtonians." The article cited a factory in Siberia that received a questionnaire from the Institute of Firebricks containing 1,487,400 questions.

The OPS went out of existence on April 30, 1953, but the price of cabbage story remained alive and well. In July 1953 a small magazine called *Cotton Picker,* published by the Automotive Booster Club of Atlanta, repeated the story. Some months later a clipping was sent to Mr. Hall at the *Washington Daily News;* it was a letter to the editor in which the writer defended the Eisenhower Administration and attacked the Truman Administration by quoting the OPS cabbage story. Seven years later, a paper called "Roll Call—The Newspaper of Capitol Hill," reprinted the story and cited a recent OPS order—even though OPS had been dead for seven years! Four years after that, the *National Observer,* a weekly newspaper, published a version of the same story, calling it "a recent federal directive" to regulate the price of cabbage. They said they got it from the *Messenger Gazette* of Somerville, New Jersey. The editor of the *Messenger Gazette* said that he did not remember where he got it, but the Concord, Massachusetts *Journal* printed the same paragraph about the recent federal directive. They said they got it from a magazine called *Quote: A Weekly Digest,* which is published in Richmond, Indiana. It also appeared in a leaflet called "Sixty-Nine-Sixty-Nine," a pamphlet put out by the Rapid Service Press, which claimed to have quoted *Quote*. The editor of *Quote* said that she got the story from a journal called, *Ties: A House Organ of the Southern Railways System*, and the *Ties* got it from the *Atlanta Journal*, where it appeared in a letter to the editor.[9] In April 1977 the item appeared in a Mobil Corporation advertising column. Walter Cronkite picked it up and mentioned it on the CBS evening news.[10] I am sure that if the federal government ever again tries to do something about prices, cabbages will roll once more.

Call-In Shows: "Not Guilty"

Recent years have brought a new phenomenon to radio known as the "call-in show." People call the "host" to comment on or ask questions about the topic of the day. In such a spontaneous format there is, of course, room for much irresponsible chatter, misinformation, and unverified news items. Not surprisingly, call-in shows have been suggested as a very common source of the kind of misinformation that starts and spreads rumors. Theoretically, all it takes is one person with a bit of misinformation for a rumor to be picked up by many listeners and spread. Consider some scenarios. In one instance, the host, who did not have a reputation for being particularly level-headed or responsible, was discussing sports and the prospects of various teams in the area. Someone called in to say that he had heard about an Oakland University (made-up name) faculty meeting in which the faculty had voted to get out of big-time athletic competition—specifically, to get out of big-time football. On hearing that, the host exclaimed to his audience, "There you have it! Oakland University has now abolished football!"[11]

A somewhat similar event occurred when a call-in host in Louisiana moderated a discussion of a proposed regulation involving the use of natural gas and coal. By the time the participants got through working over such regulations, they concluded that the people of their state were going to be forced to use coal, which they are not equipped to do either commercially or domestically, while their own natural gas was going to be shipped to the northern territories. Needless to say, a great deal of anguish was generated in this discussion.[12]

In both these instances, all the ingredients for good rumors were present, yet neither of these discussions generated any widespread rumors. Why? Perhaps the reason lies in the call-in format. In this unique communication network pattern, regular listeners have what we call a "critical self." The format provides for two-way communication, whereby the caller can talk to the host and the host can answer. Not only that, callers can talk to each other by going through the host. The network therefore is somewhat like a hub with spokes. The setup is also very amenable to self-monitoring and corrections. The listener population is usually the same; they constitute a self-contained, localized community of people. While some of them may range far from the truth in the information they pass on, there is always a good possibility that someone else will know the facts and call in immediately to rectify the error. A listener with a critical set can be very effective. Also a spokesperson for a target institution can respond quickly to allegations. In sum, I know of no instance in which a call-in show has been the source of any serious consumer rumor.

Media and Interpersonal Networks

To complete our consideration of the role of media in rumor, let us discuss the combination of media transmitting rumor and person-to-person networks. This combination is very interesting because the structure fits both the branching model and the circuit model, in that a member of the media sends out information through the branching model to groups of people who then transmit it through their own circuits. The best example of this combined format is the Satanism rumors involving McDonald's and Procter & Gamble. The subject of those rumors was of interest to certain elements of the population and to specialized media. The media contribution to the Satanist rumor transmission was based primarily on church newsletters and publications. These items were not only distributed throughout the general population but were read by other ministers and people responsible for various religious publications. Thus the item came to be included in more and more publications and proliferated in a branching fashion.

A very important part of newsletters, of course, is the letter to the editor. Many times, the Satanist story was simply a reprinting of a letter to the editor of another publication; it thus was secondary hearsay. And these letters were usually anonymous. Once the item was published in a newsletter, it was put into circulation in person-to-person circuit networks, thereby taking on the characteristics of that particular type of rumor transmission. The media story would be picked up by the congregation, who would discuss it among themselves. Procter & Gamble reported that the biggest flurries of inquiries about their alleged involvement with the Church of Satan came on Mondays.[13] This timing supports the assumption of rumor activity at church on Sundays, when people of like mind meet and get involved in person-to-person communication. Thus the newsletter was responsible for rapid and widespread dissemination of the message to groups, while person-to-person interest group circuits were responsible for elaboration of the message. Elaborations, of course, found their way back into the media networks and once again were transmitted to person-to-person networks for even more elaboration. It was in this fashion that the Satanism story became elaborated to the point that not only was the Procter & Gamble Company involved with Satanism but so was its owner, who even appeared on television to make a statement concerning his contributions and affiliations. Another elaboration involved the company's logotype: It was possible to connect the stars in such a way as to produce the ciphers "666." Other reworked versions had horns on the head of man in the moon.

The media's role in the Procter & Gamble Satanism rumor actually took the form of a technically advanced adaptation in one location, as indicated by this quotation from the *Kansas City Times*:[14]

> At the touch of a button, the word went forth from a small railroad town in Kansas. The alarm flashed along the transistorized arteries of the Union Pacific railroad's computer system and clattered out of printers along the way. "Satan is afoot," said the computer-coded cry of warning. The Procter & Gamble Company, manufacturers of Folgers coffee, Ivory Soap, Comet Cleanser, Pampers Disposable Diapers, and a supermarket full of other household products, are [Satan's] agent and should be boycotted.

It must be added that this was an unauthorized use of the Union Pacific computer system, but it was probably the most psychologically sophisticated method of transmitting warnings about the ever-growing power of Satan's empire. The use of satellites may be next.

Endnotes

1. Shibutani, Tamatso, *Improvised News* (Indianapolis: Bobbs-Merril Company, Inc., 1966).
2. Allport, Gordon, and Leo Postman, *Psychology of Rumor* (New York: Henry Holt and Company, 1947).
3. Levy, Mark R., "Watching T.V. News as Para-Social Interaction," *Journal of Broadcasting* (1979), vol. 23, pp. 69-80.
4. Koenig, Fredrick, and Gloria Lessan, "Viewers Perception of T.V. Personalities," *Psychological Reports* (in press).
5. Personal conversation with Dr. Maryhelen C. Harmon (April 7, 1978).
6. Zapp, Robert, "The Anatomy of a Rumor," distributed by E.I. du Pont de Nemours & Company, Inc.
7. Pope, John, "Contact Lens Story Impossible, Doctors Say," *New Orleans Times-Picayune/States Item* (August 4, 1983), p. 19.
8. Hall, Max, "The Great Cabbage Hoax," *Journal of Personality and Social Psychology* (1965), vol. 2, pp. 563-569.
9. Hall, Max, *op. cit.*
10. Rosnow, Ralph, and Allan Kimmel, *Psychology Today* (June 1979), pp. 58-92.
11. Personal conversation with Tom Fitzmorris (April 17, 1983).
12. Tom Fitzmorris, *op. cit.*
13. Personal conversation with William Dobson, Section Manager, Public Relations Department, The Procter & Gamble Company (July 30, 1982).
14. Hollah, William, "Firm Has a Devil of a Time with Rumor," *Kansas City Times* (July 26, 1982), p. 1.

Chapter Eight

REACTIVE RESEARCH ON RUMOR

Rumors large enough to attract widespread attention are often examined and analyzed in some fashion. Commercial rumors, especially, usually generate some kind of "in-house" accounting of what happened. Analyses can range from collecting versions of what went on from representatives in the field to full-fledged national interview surveys conducted through the company's market research operations. Whatever the extent of such efforts, they are carried on primarily for the company's own information, and few, if any, of the results are made available to the public or to interested behavioral scientists. On the other hand, the rumors discussed in this book aroused considerable outside interest, and some independent studies of them were carried out. Three of these studies will be discussed in this chapter. All three were precipitated by the problem of how commercial rumors should be combated. Specifically they question the policies of McDonald's in two of the studies and Procter & Gamble in the third.

Deworming Bulldogs

The first study was a survey research project done as a master's thesis by Susan M. Goggins at the University of Georgia in 1979.[1] This project was more pertinent than the ordinary college attitude survey because the state of Georgia was a hotbed for the McDonald's worm rumor and because the study was done shortly after that episode.

135

Goggins stated that the "purpose of the study is to evaluate the effectiveness of McDonald's tactics to squelch the
worm rumor." A survey was conducted to shed light on the
effectiveness of McDonald's advertising and publicity, the
degree of damage that was done to McDonald's reputation, and
how the rumor spread.[2] While these rather ambitious goals are
beyond the scope of a campus survey, the results of the study
are worth examination.

The investigator constructed a 24-item questionnaire. Of
these, 19 dealt in some way with McDonald's and/or the
rumor, and 5 involved demographic information (see Exhibits
8-1 and 8-2).[3] The questionnaire was not administered as a
survey interview with a one-on-one interviewer-respondent
procedure, but was given to students to be filled out in a class-
room setting before the lecture commenced. The respondents
were not a random sample at the University of Georgia but
were students who attended classes in the School of Journalism
and Mass Communications. We are not told specifically what
the courses were, but the 247 students were primarily juniors
and seniors. The surveying and sampling techniques were less
than ideal, but as the common response to this type of criticism
goes, "it is better to know something than to not know anything."

In answer to the question about where one had heard the
rumor, only 4 people said they had not heard the rumor at all
(see Exhibit 8-3).[4] The largest proportion (63 percent) said they
had heard it from a friend, which indicates that the interpersonal network accounts for most of the transmission in this
population. The remainder of the respondents who knew about
the rumor had heard or read about it through the media. The
implication clearly is that if McDonald's had not gone public
with the campaign, these people would not have heard the
rumor at all.

At first glance it would seem reasonable to be chary of engag-
ing in an anti-rumor campaign if to do so means that an additional third of the population will thereby be made aware of the
message. Without getting into epistemology, there is at least
one distinction that should be made in analyzing such a situation. The distinction between a message that makes an allegation and a message that refutes an allegation is an important
one. The latter not only counters a charge but it provides a

QUESTIONNAIRE

1. A recent rumor claimed that McDonald's puts worms in its hamburger meat. Did you become aware of the rumor from (A) a friend, (B) a radio or television *news* broadcast, (C) a newspaper *news* story, (d) an *advertisement* on radio or television, or (E) an *advertisement* in the newspaper?

    A _____ B _____ C _____ D _____ E _____

2. Do you remember seeing television or radio commercials in which McDonald's denied the rumor?

    Yes _____ No _____

3. Do you remember reading newspaper advertisements in which McDonald's denied the rumor?

    Yes _____ No _____

4. Do you remember reading news reports on radio or television about the worm rumor?

    Yes _____ No _____

5. Do you remember hearing news stories in newspapers about the worm rumor?

    Yes _____ No _____

6. Do you believe that McDonald's adds worms to its hamburger meat?

    Yes _____ No _____

7. Have you ever decided not to eat at McDonald's because of the worm rumor?

    Yes _____ No _____

8. After you heard the rumor, did you pass it on to someone else?

    Yes _____ No _____

9. Has your overall image of McDonald's been worsened because of the rumor?

    Yes _____ No _____

Exhibit 8-1

QUESTIONNAIRE

1. Please rate each statement on a scale of 1 to 5.   1. Strongly Agree
    Answer by placing the appropriate numbers in   2. Agree
    spaces provided to the right of each statement.   3. Undecided
                                                         4. Disagree
                                                         5. Strongly Disagree

10. Small firms are more trustworthy than big corporations like
     McDonald's.   _____

11. Information you get from friends is more trustworthy than
     information that comes from radio, television, and newspapers.   _____

12. Advertisements are more trustworthy than news stories and
     broadcasting.   _____

13. News stories and broadcasts are more trustworthy than
     advertisements.   _____

14. Food additives are a serious problem that everyone should be
     concerned about.

15. McDonald's denial of the rumor means that the rumor is true.   _____

16. When McDonald's did not deny the rumor when it first came out,
     that made it look as if the rumor were true.   _____

17. The fact that McDonald's never actually mentioned the worm
     rumor in its advertisements was confusing.   _____

18. Rank the items below 1 through 9 in order of their importance in
     influencing your belief or non belief in the rumor:

     Your own knowledge   _____

     television commercials   _____

     radio commercials   _____

     newspaper advertisements _____

     television news   _____

     radio news   _____

     newspaper news stories   _____

     the rumor itself   _____

     talks with friends   _____

19. If you first heard the rumor from a friend, where did they say they heard it?

     _____

     Please answer the following questions about yourself:

21. Class: Freshman ___ Sophomore ___ Junior ___ Senior ___ Graduate ___

22. Sex: Male ___ Female ___

23. Age: ___

24. Race: ___

25. Home town: ___

Exhibit 8-2

	N=	%
A friend	156	63.2
A radio or television news broadcast	67	27.1
A newspaper story	12	4.9
An advertisement on radio or television	8	3.2
Did not hear the rumor	4	1.6
An advertisement in the newspaper	0	0

Exhibit 8-3   Where respondents first heard the rumor

different motivational setting for the message to be passed on through the networks.

The questionnaire also asked where the friend had heard the rumor. Forty percent said they heard it from another friend; 45 percent said their friends heard it from a media source; and 15 percent said they did not know where their friends had picked it up. The implication is that 45 percent of the friends would not have known the rumor had it not been for the media campaign. However, we do not know which version of the message the friends received. Also, lending too much credence to the "respondent's recollection of his friend's recollection" is dubious. As we pointed out in an earlier chapter, one component of many rumors is a "source" for credibility, and in contemporary commercial rumors the source tends to be a television program.

The next series of results deal with questions on recall of advertising and publicity (Exhibit 8-4).[5] Electronic media seem to have had the most impact on the students via both commercials and news stories. New stories were remembered more often than commercials, even though there were many more commercials than news items. These results call forth several observations. Only 3.5 percent of the respondents recognized any validity at all in the worm allegation six months or so after the rumor/anti-rumor period; essentially the rumor had been squelched. However, 57 percent said they had passed on the rumor after they heard it. How many heard it as message one or message two? How many of the 57 percent disbelieved the rumor at the time they heard it, but passed it on anyway? Such items should have been in the questionnaire. (Monday morning

Question	Yes	No	Not Sure
Do you remember hearing news reports on radio or television about the rumor?	68.7%	31.3%	—
Do you remember hearing television or radio commercials in which McDonald's denied the rumor?	64.7%	35.3%	—
Do you remember reading news stories in the newspaper about the worm rumor?	38.2%	61.8%	—
Do you remember reading newspaper advertisements in which McDonald's denied the rumor?	24.9%	75.1%	—
Do you believe McDonald's adds worms to hamburgers?	2.4%	96.4%	1.2%
Have you ever decided not to eat at McDonald's because of the worm rumor?	8.4%	91.6%	—
After you heard the rumor, did you pass it on to someone else?	57.4%	42.6%	—
Has your overall image of McDonald's been worsened because of the rumor?	8.4%	91.2%	0.4%

Exhibit 8-4   Advertising/publicity recall plus impact of the rumor

quarterbacking is no less popular with research than it is with sports.)

While only 3.6 percent were not convinced of the falsity of the worm additive message, over twice that many admitted to having the content of the allegation actually affect their behavior—that is, influence them not to eat at McDonald's. This figure is certainly understated; believing one thing and acting in an opposite manner is a form of nonrational behavior that many people prefer not to acknowledge. Also, the negative image suggested by the rumor could exist at various levels of consciousness and could lead one to get a pizza or a taco without being aware of why one did so.

When participants were asked to rank sources that influenced their disbelief in the rumor, television news was ranked first; an ambiguous category, "my own knowledge," was ranked second; and radio news was third. The author's overall conclusion was that McDonald's anti-rumor campaign was effective.

Watching Wildcats in a Cage

A study called, "Using Information Processing Theory to Design Marketing Strategies,"[6] was ostensibly carried out to demonstrate the applicability of information theory to marketing. Our interest here lies not in information theory per se but in the substantive findings of the investigation. That concern of the study was McDonald's response to the question of what to do about the worm rumor. The preliminary assumption of this study was that the public refutation campaign was a failure—a rather curious position because it was based on one newspaper column dealing with an interview with one McDonald's official in Ohio a few weeks after the counter-rumor campaign began.[7] Whatever the questionable assumptions precipitating the research, however, the study is worth examining in its own right.

The approach to this research was that of a controlled laboratory experiment, a setup quite different from that of the previously cited survey. As any behavioral scientist will tell you, there are definite advantages to the rigor of a controlled experiment, but these are frequently offset by the difficulty of applying "behavior in a cage" to the "real world." This problem will become apparent as we evaluate the results.

The researchers started out by couching McDonald's problem in information theory terms:[8]

> *Individuals exposed to a rumor linking the object, McDonald's, to an attribute, worms, store this association in memory. Subsequent evaluation of the object requires retrieval of object-relevant thoughts from memory. Among the thoughts retrieved is the one produced by the rumor and possibly others related to the attribute specified by the rumor. Because these thoughts are less positive than those that would have been retrieved in the absence of the rumor, the evaluation of the object is less favorable. Consumers are affected because they process the rumor, not because they necessarily believe it.*

In other words people hearing the worm rumor will have unpleasant feelings about McDonald's hamburgers whether they believe the rumor or not. They also say that refutation of the allegation, "McDonald's does not contain worms," merely strengthens the association between McDonald's and worms.[9] (Actually the McDonald's campaign was very careful to avoid using the term "worms" for that very reason.)

The investigators suggested two strategies to deal with the problem of negative association or "residue." One they called a "storage strategy," which involved the following:[10]

> ... *introducing a second object at the time rumor information is stored. The presence of the second object is intended to foster the association of the rumor attribute with that object rather than with the object (McDonald's) initially specified in the rumor. Moreover, if the second object is positively evaluated by rumor recipients, some of this effect is likely to become associated with the rumor attribute (worms), making it less negative. Hence, even if the rumor attribute is still associated with the initial object (McDonald's), it will not have as adverse an effect on that object's evaluation as would be the case in the absence of the storage strategy.*

They meant that if there is additional information that makes the "worm allegation" of the rumor seem appealing it will negate the offensive connection between hamburgers and worms.

The other strategy, called "retrieval strategy," was based on the notion that judicious "choice of a stimulus will direct retrieval of thoughts in memory away from rumor-stimulated associations. Even if the new stimulus does not completely inhibit the retrieval of object-rumor attribute associations, it is likely to dilute these associations with other thoughts in active memory."[11] It is a form of diversionary tactic whereby a positive association is made with the target of the rumor to counter the negative association.

In order to test the two strategies, 64 graduate students were recruited as subjects. They were told to view and evaluate a television program, with commercials interspersed to simulate actual viewing conditions. Because the commercials might influence overall response to the program, the students were asked to evaluate the commercials also. Of the twelve commercials, three were about McDonald's; these were presented at the beginning, middle, and end of the film. Three forms of independent variables were contrived. A "rumor" was planted by having a confederate (ostensibly a research participant) announce at the end of the third McDonald's commercial, "You know these McDonald's commercials remind me of that rumor about worms and McDonald's—you know, that McDonald's uses worm meat in their hamburgers."[12] The third condition was the control trials in which no rumor was mentioned and the confederate was present merely as a participant.

One of the "cue" conditions was manipulated by having the experimenter say after the rumor announcement, "That may sound funny to you, but last week when my mother-in-law was in town we took her to the Chez Paul and had a really good sauce made out of worms." (This is an example of storage strategy.)[13]

The other cue was introduced by administering some questions to which the subjects wrote answers concerning the location of the McDonald's they frequent most often, how often they visit it a year, and whether or not it had indoor seating. The idea was to stimulate retrieval of thoughts about McDonald's other than the ones related to the worm rumor. (This is an example of retrieval strategy.)[14]

Another situation was staged to simulate the "McDonald's response" to the rumor. The experimenter reacted to the confederate's announcement about the worms by saying, "That is just not true. If nothing else, worms are too expensive—$8.00 a pound! Besides, the FDA did a study and found that McDonald's uses 100% pure beef."[15]

The dependent variables were measured by having subjects rate on a seven-point scale items about McDonald's with respect to "good-quality food/bad-quality food," "completely fits my needs/does not fit my needs at all," and "certain to eat at McDonald's/certain not to eat at McDonald's." The subject scores were added up to produce a total "evaluative index," and the results are depicted in Exhibit 8-5. Planting the rumor was obviously effective in that people evaluated McDonald's less favorably when the rumor was announced than when it was not (see part (a) of Exhibit 8-5.) However, refuting the statement about the worms did not appear to have an effect: The ratings were the same for the rumor alone as for the rumor followed by the refutation (see Exhibit 8-5 (c).) Both the storage strategy and the retrieval strategy appear to be effective in counteracting the rumor message, and to about the same degree.

The results are impressive in that they indicate the influence of association on the resulting impact of a negative message. The suggestion that worms were palatable obviously defused the "ugh factor" of the worm additive suggestion, although the

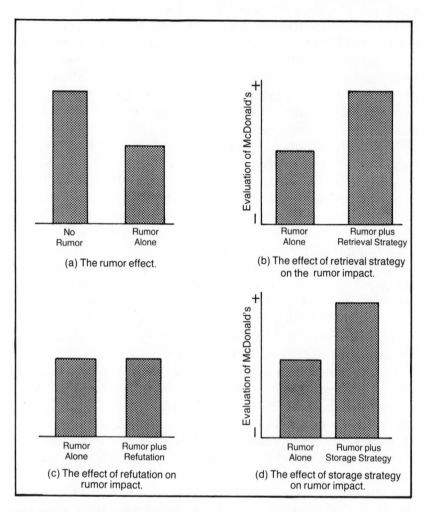

Exhibit 8-5   **Results of preparing an evaluative index.**

practical applications of such a strategy may be questionable. A relatively sophisticated population such as Northwestern students has probably had direct or indirect experience with exotic foods. They have probably traveled to Europe and eaten snails, squid, and mussels. If nothing else they have at least seen packages of "novelty items" such as chocolate-covered bees in local gourmet food shops; accordingly they ought to be more receptive to suggestions about "Chez Paul's worm sauce" than the general population.

The other tactic of stimulating positive associations with the target worked out quite well, and this approach is certainly something that can be implemented in an actual public relations program. Such a program could emphasize the neatness and cleanliness of the establishments, the general pleasant ambiance of the settings, and the fond memories people have of gathering there.

The importance of association is further emphasized by observing the results of the experimental treatment using a refutation. Obviously, stating that "they do not put worms in their hamburgers" does not detract from the "ugh factor" of the message and probably tends to strengthen the association of McDonald's. In all fairness to the efforts of McDonald's Corporate Communications Department, it should be emphasized that what is termed in the article as the "worming-out" refutational strategy used by McDonald's" was not ever used by them. They scrupulously avoided the term "worms" in any of their messages, and they never stated that worms cost eight dollars a pound and were too expensive to use. The implication that a repulsive additive is more expensive than the meat itself does not do much for the image one is trying to maintain. In fact the approach used by McDonald's was very similar to what was termed in the study "retrieval strategy." They would emphasize the positive image of McDonald's by having full-page color advertisements of the most beautiful looking hamburger one has ever seen, with the caption "100% pure government inspected beef."

As interesting as this research report is, it is a study of attitude formation and attitude changes, not of rumors as such. As we pointed out earlier, rumors involve a process of passing on a message through networks. An anti-rumor campaign not only tries to correct the misinformation in the original message but also tries to *stop* the message from being passed on. There is nothing in this study that deals with reduced motivation to pass the message on to somebody else. The experiment does not address the multiple factors involved in the two-step flow of communication in interpersonal networks. Presumably, on the basis of what has been discussed earlier, a rumor moves up from a marginal, low-status member of the group. However, news moves into the network from a highly credible opinion leader. Rumor refutations are "news" and should have different dynamics than rumors themselves. These complexities could not be included in the type of experimental design used in this study.

The results were based on attitudes that were measured immediately after the various experimental treatments were made. It would be of interest to know how people would respond after a longer period of time had elapsed. Some 47 of the subjects were interviewed two days later and asked if they believed the rumor. Essentially they did not, but it would be interesting to know how they would have scored on the three "attractiveness scales" two days later, and even two weeks later.

Advertising Age Proctors a Gamble

On page one of the August 9th, 1982 issue of *Advertising Age* there appeared a feature story with the headline, "Procter & Gamble Rumor Blitz Looks Like a Bomb."[16] The tenor of the story was that, after examining all facets of the case, they considered Procter & Gamble's campaign ill-advised and poorly handled. Part of their argument was based on a national survey. The publication commissioned the SRI Research Center of Lincoln, Nebraska to conduct a nationwide telephone survey of a sample of 1,264 Americans 18 years of age or over. The poll was conducted from July 29th through August 3rd, 1982.

An aspect of the rumor that piqued the curiosity of *Advertising Age* was a regional comparison of the South with the nation as a whole. Some of the results worth noting were that 32 percent of all Americans were aware of the rumors, and 42 percent of the people in the South knew about them. About 3 percent of the respondents said they believed the rumors, while in the South 5 percent said they believed them. Nationally 21 percent said they "weren't sure," while in the South 27 percent were doubtful.[17]

How did the rumor affect purchasing? Of those who believed the rumor or said they were not sure, 17 percent said they were curtailing their purchases of Procter & Gamble products. Only 5 percent of the people who were aware of the rumor (1.6 of all respondents) said they were buying fewer products, and 1 percent said they were buying more. One point the authors of the article were trying to make was that the rumor was not a problem as far as sales were concerned. In fact the survey showed that 79 percent of the people interviewed did not know what products Procter & Gamble makes; thus, any attempt at an organized boycott would have been difficult.

Their conclusion that the campaign was unnecessary was not well-founded. There are reasons other than sales for Procter & Gamble or any other corporation to decide to launch an anti-rumor campaign. Answering all the questions that come in concerning a rumor may become a burden, and not doing anything may project an image of the corporation as being weak and ineffectual and of the public relations director as being indecisive.

Endnotes

1. Goggins, Susan M., *The Wormburger Scare* (Athens, Georgia: University of Georgia, 1978), unpublished master's thesis.
2. Goggins, *op. cit.*, p. 3.
3. Goggins, *op. cit.*, pp. 65, 66.
4. Goggins, *op. cit.*, p. 35.
5. Goggins, *op. cit.*, p. 36.
6. Tybout, Alice M., Bobby J. Calber, and Brian Sternthal, "Using Information Processing Theory to Design Marketing Strategies," *Journal of Marketing Research*, Vol. 18 (1981), pp. 73-79.
7. Greene, Bob, "Trying to Unravel a Can of Worms," *Washington Star* (November 24, 1978), p. 32.
8. Tybout, *op. cit.*, p. 74.
9. Tybout, *op. cit.*, p. 74.
10. Tybout, *op. cit.*, p. 75.
11. Tybout, *op. cit.*, p. 75.
12. Tybout, *op. cit.*, p. 75.
13. Tybout, *op. cit.*, p. 76.
14. Tybout, *op. cit.*, p. 76.
15. Tybout, *op. cit.*, p. 76.
16. "Procter & Gamble Rumor Blitz Looks Like a Bomb," *Advertising Age* (August 9, 1982).
17. "Procter & Gamble," *op. cit.*, p. 1.

Chapter Nine

RUMOR AND THE
STOCK MARKET PLACE

Although it is a different setting from most of our previous subjects, Wall Street—like other financial centers—is certainly a
market, and rumors are a frequent phenomenon there. Dan
Rotbart of the *Wall Street Journal* says, "Wall Street loves
rumors, even though most of them aren't worth the breath it
takes to pass them along."[1] Indeed, just a glance through the
September 13, 1984 *Wall Street Journal* (Southwest edition)
reveals a prevalence of rumors and suggests their importance:

> *"Shop Talk—Odds and Ends"... Once a rumor gets started it can
> become virtually indestructible. That's the case with a rumor that
> Campbell Soup Company and General Foods Corporation have
> been talking about a merger (page 29).*
> *Imperial Group Gains on Takeover Rumors ... Investors buy-
> ing Imperial Group shares and figuring it's case of "heads-I-win,
> tails I do not lose." Rumors of a possible takeover bid or a re-
> shuffling of assets have been swirling around the British Tobacco
> Company, which has diversified into food, beer, restaurants, and
> lodging ("Heard on the Street," Maile Hulihan, p. 53).*
> *Bylaws Changes at May Department Stores Fuel Purchase
> Rumors ... Saint Louis—May Department Store Company
> holders approved changes to the company's bylaws that fuel spec-
> ulation that the nation's third largest department store chain may
> be considering an acquisition. Rumors recently have circulated
> that May wants to buy Carson Pirie Scott & Company, a
> Chicago-based retailer—a purchase that would make May a force
> in a new market and bring in some operations such as catering
> and business (John Curley, page 54).*

Market observers have told me that people there thrive and
traffic on rumors and that the market feeds on rumors and

trades on them. Some are positive, some are negative, but they can affect the stock, bond, or commodity markets, causing them to move up and down.[2] One broker told me that rumors on Wall Street are "just like those everywhere else," but I am skeptical of that statement. Certainly some of them are similar to those elsewhere in that they are small, trivial, and interesting but not necessarily consequential. Stock market rumors, however, more than any other rumor phenomenon, have the potential capacity not only to *attract* attention among the population in which they are circulated but also to have serious *effects* on that same population. Two recent separate, but related, events in which rumors played a part illustrate the point.

Doing the Continental

The first case involved Continental Illinois Bank of Chicago, a fascinating history to unravel because it is an entanglement of strings of realities and rumors. People in the business world frequently point to Continental as a prime example of a company that was done in by rumors. Just as often, people will say that Continental was *not* done in by rumors but by trouble of its own making, and that the hearsay merely reflected that fact.[3] No matter which version one hears, rumors are always part of the account. It was no secret that Continental had troubles. It had bought some 2 billion dollars in loans from Penn Square Bank in Oklahoma, and when Penn Square went under, most of the loans became worthless. The ensuing concern and speculation were not relieved by the knowledge that the bank also had made 3 to 4 billion dollars in loans to third world countries—loans which might not be repaid. People connected with the bank were jittery, and people in the general market, if not jittery, were at least very interested in what might happen. All of this background made Continental a susceptible target for hearsay.[4]

Reporters pick out May 8, 1984 as the critical day for Continental's crisis, but bits and pieces of "talk" preceded that date. For a few days, word went around that Continental was on the verge of bankruptcy and was about to file under Chapter 11.[5] The frivolity of that chatter is plain when one stops to reflect that banks do not go bankrupt, nor can they file under Chapter 11. Obviously the hearsay was circulating among people who had limited knowledge of, or involvement in, the banking and finance industry. Nonetheless, Continental was the subject of tales. When its treasurer, Robert McKnew, was quoted on Reuters and Dow Jones News Services as denying "the preposterous rumors," the corporation's problems were brought more into view. What has been singled out as the most significant event of May 8th was the story filed by Toshio Aritake, a Japanese reporter in the New York Bureau of the Commodity News Service, who had picked up some items from the rumor mill churning around Continental. As described by the Chicago *Tribune* on Sunday, May 27, 1984, "At about 3:50 p.m. on Thursday May 8th, (he) ... finished writing a story on the possibility that a Japanese financial institution might be buying Continental Illinois Bank. He punched the 'send' key on his computer terminal and the story moved to CNS clients around the world." Aritake named three big Japanese firms that were hoping to buy or buy into the bank, according to "banking sources." He went on to say that the three concerns were "rumored to be approaching Continental about a takeover." Later Aritake said that the source for his four-paragraph story was "rumors" gathered by telephone. It was May 9th when the CNS story hit Tokyo. Jiji, a Japanese News Agency, has the right to use and transmit CNS stories that come to its country. In translating the story, Jiji made it sound much more solid than a rumor when it ran, "A bank source in New York *disclosed* ..." The shorter, more emphatic version went out on the wires not only to media but also to financial houses. Jiji's account alone would have been enough. Shortly after that message, however, the Reuters story about rumors and denials came in; the panic started and a run on the bank began in Japan. Whatever the rumor problem might have been, the "panic problem" followed the sun to the European financial capitals, then to New York and Chicago. The actions that ensued involved rescuing the United States banking system from a domestic disaster as well as saving the White House for the Republican incumbent.

The Problem Spreads

The events at Continental Illinois caused a general sense of uneasiness and lack of confidence about U.S. financial institutions. Market watchers and players became anxious about the ability of banks to get back money they had loaned. Although Continental's problems originated several years ago with domestic loans, its crisis was linked to a foreign cutoff of money. That danger, together with the Persian Gulf crisis and the fact that *many* banks were sitting on loans from Argentina, Mexico, and other third world countries, made stock prices drop for banking companies during that period.[6] The bank whose stock dropped the most was Manufacturers Hanover (down $3\frac{3}{8}$ points). This drop, plus the knowledge that the bank had a heavy exposure to Latin American borrowers, may have been enough to single it out as a rumor target. On May 24th in London, word was out that "Manny Hanny" could not fund itself and was liquidating its portfolio of British government bonds called "gilts." The people at Manufacturers Hanover, however, had an easier time with their rumor problem than had Continental a few weeks earlier. For one thing, this bank had earned a large amount of money in the previous year, its 12th consecutive year of record earnings. This history made stories about its troubles less credible. The rumor itself was also very specific, which made it easier to refute. At 10:30 a.m. Manufacturers Hanover sent a denial to all the wire services, pointing out that they had no position on gilts and therefore could not be selling them. Between noon and 1 p.m. things returned to normal. Michael O'Neil of corporate communications for the bank felt that the initial problem was a "sign of the times" reaction but that there were enough people who had sufficient background information to judge the realities of the situation, especially when the denial of the gilts ownership came over the Dow-Jones "board tape."[7]

Categories of Market Rumors

Are rumors on Wall Street different from rumors elsewhere? If so, in what way do they differ? How does previous rumor research help us in understanding what goes on in the business community?

Much of the work done on rumors reflects the nature of the particular message and the carrying population studied. Rumors are routed through groups for whom the message is relevant. Sometimes a rumor is of general interest to the entire community, but others circulate within special groups and spread from group to group. This group-to-group kind of transmission has been accelerated incredibly by the electronic communications revolution.

The purpose of classifying rumors is not to identify "real types" of rumors but, instead, to find the most useful way of arranging them for purposes of analysis. Rumors in the financial market appear to have two dimensions: They can be *public* or *market*, and they can be relevant to the *general* financial market or to a *special* segment of it. (See Exhibit 9-1). In February of 1984 there was a rumor that President Reagan had suffered a heart attack. Although the word was primarily passed through Wall Street, it was the sort of thing that would interest everybody—that is, *the public.* On the other hand, speculation about the takeover of Chicago-based Jewel Corporation in May of 1984 was relevant to the financial community rather than to the public; thus, it was a *market* rumor. Within the market the Reagan item was of *general* relevance, while the Jewel Corporation takeover had relevance to a *special* group. The Continental Illinois reports were of market interest for the most part but were relevant to the *general* financial community. One summer's rumors of rainstorms and flooding in the Midwest were of *public* concern, but they caused action also among a *specific group,* grain speculators.

Rumors are a particularly persistent problem in the financial world because all action there is based on information. Advance information thus can be important in terms of profits and losses. As one market expert stated, "The traders' jungle

	PUBLIC	MARKET
GENERAL	Reagan has a heart attack	Continental Illinois collapse.
SPECIFIC	Rain storms and flooding in the Midwest.	Jewel Corporation takeover.

Exhibit 9-1   Categories of financial rumors.

drums are among the most sensitive in the world." One can gamble that information is true, but even if it is unverified, it can be "real" in its consequences. A couple of years ago a rumor circulated that the U.S. Consulate in Warsaw was under siege—a spin-off from the then Iranian hostage jitters. It was not true, but for a brief spell the price of gold shot up, and a few people made a profit. More than in any other area of modern life, in the financial world rumors have to be treated as an actuality in their own right. Barry Schneider, news editor of the Commodity News Service, was interviewed about the Continental Illinois problems. He said, "Our policy regarding rumors is that if they're just talk, we try to stay away from them. But if they are affecting trading, you can't just ignore them."[8]

Anatomy of Wall Street Rumor

An example of the intricacy and sensitivity of the market network was documented by a case study called, "The Anatomy of a Rumor on Wall Street."[9] The rumor centered on the activities of a Merrill Lynch analyst who specialized in IBM stock. What happened to that stock seems to be important to the stock market in general:[10]

> *Perhaps more than any other publicly held stock, Wall Street pays close attention to IBM. The computer company's stock is owned by more institutional investors than any other, and IBM is an important component in a variety of market indexes, including the Dow Jones Industrial Average and Standard & Poor's Corp. 100-stock index. Many investors adjust their outlooks on the market as a whole—and technology stocks in particular—based on IBM's earnings performance and the price fluctuations of its shares.*

People on Wall Street were interested in whether or not IBM could continue its long-term growth at the current pace. For some time, its annual rate had been 15 percent, but in the previous three quarters it had risen to 22 percent. There was speculation that the company would not maintain this pace in the fourth quarter, but would approach the previous norm by dropping to some extent. Mr. Rotbart's account in the *Wall Street Journal* goes on . . .:[11]

> *Against that backdrop came the rumor that Merrill Lynch's Mr. Mandresh—who concedes that he's one of the most bullish*

IBM analysts—was going to lower his fourth-quarter estimate or change his longstanding "strong buy" recommendation on the stock. As the rumor fanned out on Tuesday, October 16, IBM's stock, which had been up, fell back almost two points. It later rebounded after Mr. Mandresh's denial, but finished the day down 1¼ points.

Although Merrill Lynch took credit for squelching the rumor, the fact that it existed at all was probably one of those instances in which there was a kernel of truth in the story. Mr. Mandresh had been saying for most of the year that IBM's 1984 earnings would be $10.50 to $10.75 a year. On October 11th he looked at the day's earnings and announced to the Merrill Lynch sales force that he had revised his estimate and that he no longer felt that a "range estimate" was appropriate. He would go with its upper end and say that estimated earnings would be at $10.75. The next day he received a "not so fast, Dan" admonition from some people at IBM:[12]

By his own account, Mr. Mandresh spoke to his sources at IBM the next day. In their characteristically vague way, they warned him that his "new" estimate might be too high. The IBM sources indicated to him that three variables were likely to contribute to lower profitability: a larger drag on foreign operations' results because of the strong dollar; a higher tax rate than in the third quarter; and a possible decline in gross margins. After his talks with his IBM contacts, Mr. Mandresh says it was clear to him that his estimates of the company's earnings "aren't in the piggybank."

There followed a four-day period between October 12th and October 16th when Merrill Lynch's large institutional clients were told of some misgivings at IBM concerning Mandresh's prediction for the fourth quarter:[13]

Mr. Mandresh "definitely realized (that IBM's full-year earnings) won't be $10.75 a share," says a large institutional client who spoke with Mr. Mandresh the day before he publicly denied the rumor. "To those who were aware of it," the client says, Mr. Mandresh's "informal change ... was almost as significant as if he had formally reduced his estimate."

Another client, who works for a firm that owns more than a million IBM shares, concluded from a conversation with Mr. Mandresh that the analyst had, in effect, lowered his earnings estimate. "I would say he might have backpedaled 10 cents a share this year," the client says.

Meanwhile thousands of the salespeople affiliated with Merrill Lynch were telling individual small-scale clients the first message, that IBM would close the fourth quarter at $10.75.

It is easy to see how rumors can thrive in such an atmosphere of mixed messages, ambiguity, and questionable credibility, where a broker gives one message to one group of clients and a different message to another group.

When people are densely packed together in a supercharged atmosphere where millions of dollars are won or lost on hunches, predictions, and guesses based on good and bad information, you are obviously going to find a high collective anxiety quotient. Dealing rapidly in futures and selling is a very high pressure endeavor. One would expect universal and local-specific rumors to be a large factor in commodity trading. Here is a sample of those important enough to make headings in the *New York Times* financial section.

> *Grains and Soybeans Rise on Foreign-Sale Rumor (November 13, 1981)*
>
> *Rumor of Oil Embargo Sends Oil Futures Up (June 10, 1981)*
>
> *Sugar Prices Sour Again on Rumor of Purchases (May 30, 1981)*
>
> *Rumor of Hostage Deal Weakens Futures Prices (January 10, 1981)*
>
> *Precious Metals Rise on Rumors from Iran (July 23, 1980)*
>
> *Hostage Release Rumors Push Gold Futures Down (October 18, 1980)*
>
> *Rumors of Rain Send Most Grain Prices Down (July 16, 1980)*
>
> *Frost Rumors Lift Coffee (June 27, 1980)*
>
> *Sugar at a Record Close on Soviet-Buying Rumor (November 24, 1979)*
>
> *Rumors on Iran Crisis Feed Gold Futures Rise (December 5, 1979)*
>
> *Wheat Soybeans Rise on Soviet Buying Rumors (June 7, 1979)*
>
> *Silver Gains on Rumors of Possible Big Delivery (January 24, 1979)*

In sum, J.H. Maidenberg, commodities columnist for the *New York Times*, says, "Rumor has always been as strong an influence on prices of commodities as fact."[14]

The "Whys" of Market Rumors

While anxiety seems to be a cause of rumors on the financial scene, actual fear is less so. As we have seen, rumors can substantiate one's fears, justify one's antagonistic feelings, or confirm one's world view. If fear is shared by others, hearsay can be used to reinforce a group position and to maintain solidarity. When, for example, a group of people fear the "Moonies" or communists or feel that takeover by the forces of Satan is imminent, they will welcome and circulate among the like-minded any report which bears out their contention.

This type of reaction is rare on Wall Street. To be sure, there are some people who believe that Third World loans are going to blow up the banking system, and indeed those fears may have played a part in the bank rumors of May 1984. And there are apocalyptical traders and hoarders who spread stories about imminent doom. Nevertheless, I do not think that fear plays as important a role in the financial market as it does in other rumor scenes.

What *does* play a big part on Wall Street is rumor as a substitute for news. In a population where information is essential, what is not available is often invented. This tendency is especially true for local items. Because information is critical, everyone is operating with high-powered antenna. In this tense atmosphere the population is sensitized to a bit of news here, a piece of a report there. People under stress need closure, order, a feeling of completion; they need to put pieces together so that they can make sense of the whole. The media often fail to provide such closure, and ordinary means of verification cannot always keep pace with all that is heard. So when bits and pieces of information are bouncing around Wall Street, people often fill in the gaps by speculating. When such speculation is communicated, it becomes rumor.

Of course, the message must be interesting and relevant; there must be some reason to focus on the topic. The selection of a target for allegations is more easily explained on Wall Street than elsewhere. Usually there are events surrounding a corporation that stimulate conjecture about what is going on. For example, in June 1984 there was talk about St. Regis Paper Company being for sale. Australian publisher Rupert Murdoch, who was in the market for paper companies, said he had taken a "position," but he would not comment on St. Regis. When the St. Regis people also "declined to comment," there were wide gaps for people to fill with their own fantasies.[15]

In another instance, the market was buzzing about Toyota and General Motors getting together to build a small car. This rumor was sparked by the two chairmen dining together in New York. Talk was spurred on by the *Wall Street Journal,* which said: "Both companies are keeping relatively tight lips and the few public comments they have made seem only to heighten the confusion."[16] Similarly, in Chicago Jewel Corporation was the subject of "takeover chatter" when its chairman met with the head of another chain store outfit and they then refused comment.[17]

Rumors are short-lived in the financial world, however, because everything there is supercharged and more active than elsewhere. More people are involved in passing information in a short period of time. Also, it is important for people to get at the truth one way or another and to verify a message or discount it. In situations away from Wall Street there is usually not as much pressure on the participating population to discover the truth, nor does the target of the story usually feel the same sense of urgency. The rumor about Procter & Gamble's connection to the Church of Satan, for instance, went on for three years. The population involved in the telling did not want to have the situation clarified because the rumor suited their view of things—that is, that Satan is a real threat to Christians. For the target, Procter & Gamble, the story was a mild annoyance but was not hurting sales.

On Wall Street, events themselves usually clarify information as being true or false very quickly. Speculations that circulate for more than a few weeks are usually a string of repeated tales set up by continuing ambiguous circumstances. For example, the possibility of a merger between Campbell Soup Company and General Foods circulated for several months during the summer of 1984. The rumor persisted because representatives from the two corporations continued to meet. Only when they announced that they were negotiating about a frozen food batter patent that Campbell wanted to buy from General Foods Corporation did the merger speculation stop.[18] Financial rumors are short-lived also because Wall Street people can sense what is real and what is not, and they know how to get verification quickly from Washington, New York, or anywhere in the world.

Where do Wall Street tales come from? Some say they start

on the trading floor, while others say they begin in the commodity exchange in Chicago. A trader in Chicago says that they begin in neither of these places but, rather, in the international money centers, and that a phone call from Madrid or Budapest can set them off here.[19] The structural theory of transmission argues that messages go from the bottom of a hierarchy to the top, reinforcing the idea that rumors start on "the floor." Possibly more important is the fact that the trading floor of the exchange is an environment wherein a higher concentration of people are subjected to more incomplete information bits flying around than anywhere else. In such a frenetic atmosphere, the factors that link anxiety and rumor behavior—the need to provide closure and the tendency to listen to conjecture—are maximized.

The international aspect of rumor is also interesting. Very little work has been done on world-wide rumors, but they certainly do exist in matters of finance. The Continental Illinois saga showed that stories follow the sun. The time differential seems important because an information bit can go to San Francisco after the East Coast and Midwest exchanges are closed, then move on to Tokyo, Hong Kong, Budapest, Milan, and London. Meanwhile the sources of verification are closed for the night, allowing the rumor to generate more speculation and to gather strength, much like an off-shore hurricane.

A speculative tale will stop if another version fills in the gaps and makes more sense. An official at the Securities and Exchange Commission tells about the CEO whose secretary told callers he could not talk to them because he had gone to Pittsburgh. Talk began about Mellon, mergers, and the like. Actually the man had gone home for Mother's Day—an explanation that was finally accepted, but not before the stock had dropped.

Perhaps this episode should have provided a lesson for the company president whose stock had been going up and down. Because he was not going to be at an important consumer electronics show in Chicago, he issued a form letter to a handful of select reporters: "Hello, ...: I will not be at the C.E.S. due to the graduation of my daughter from Princeton. I do hope that you will drop by the Atari booth." The tactic seemed to work. On June 20th the *Wall Street Journal* ran a story about it with the heading, "Squelching Rumors Before They Start."

Dealing with Market Rumors

As I said, most financial rumors are short-lived, but they can survive long enough to upset things, causing short-term ups and downs. They continue to exist as long as they provide an explanation for what is happening or what is going to happen. One way to stop a rumor is to deny it and provide a *better* explanation. Besides satisfying the need for closure, the explanation will also reduce motivation for spreading the story on the part of attention-seeking individuals, because the matter has been made public and the rumor version has been refuted. However, the denial and response have to be more credible than the hearsay. It does no good for the captain of a ship to issue denials about its sinking if water is pouring into the stateroom and the ship is listing at a 45-degree angle. When Manufacturers Hanover was being bad-mouthed, they made a forthright public statement to all key media representatives that the rumor was not true, that they did not own "gilts" and that they were in good shape. The public knowledge that their financial situation was strong made their statement credible.

In another instance, Hawaii Savings and Loan faced a run by depositors when two Hawaiian industrial loan companies were closed by state officials. The word about their insolvency became generalized to include Hawaii S & L. The bank denied the rumor, stating that they could pay back all deposits and staying open past closing time to instill confidence in their solvency. (One branch stayed open until 10 p.m.). Executives mingled with the crowds of depositors, assuring them of the safety of their deposits. Television monitors were set up in the lobbies to telecast reports of the run and official denials of the rumored closings. In sum, the rumor was refuted and the run was stopped.[20] In contrast to this situation, the messages from Continental Illinois emanated from various sources and were often confusing. Also, the company's problems with loans had been known for some time.

Rumors in the financial world will probably continue, or even become more prevalent. The Volker monetary policy has made it a "real time" market, and stress, anxiety, and bombardment of disparate pieces of information will continue to cause conjecture. But some measures could be enacted to reduce their disturbing effects. For example, it is possible to set up rumor control centers for quick call checkouts on stories. This procedure would be particularly valuable in countering the "information lag" that accompanies the international "follow the sun" stories.

It may also be feasible to train people to be discriminating in what they believe. The same rumors continue to circulate—only the names are different. We need to be able to distinguish what is valid from what is not valid in classrooms, board rooms and stock exchanges, too.

Endnotes

1. Rotbart, Dean, "Anatomy of a Rumor on Wall Street," *Wall Street Journal* (October 26, 1984).
2. Official at Securities and Exchange Commission, personal interview (August 15, 1984).
3. Shellenbarger, Sue, *Wall Street Journal* reporter, personal interview (August 16, 1984).
4. Metz, Tim, *Wall Street Journal* reporter, personal interview (September 5, 1984).
5. *New York Times* (May 9, 1984).
6. O'Neil, Michael, Head of Corporate Communications Manufacturers, personal interview at Hanover Corporation (September 6, 1984).
7. O'Neil, Michael, *op. cit.*
8. Longworth, R.C., and Bill Bamhart, "The Run on Continental," *Chicago Tribune* (May 27, 1984).
9. Rotbart, *op. cit.*
10. Rotbart, *op. cit.*
11. Rotbart, *op. cit.*
12. Rotbart, *op. cit.*
13. Rotbart, *op. cit.*
14. Maidenberg, J.H., "Commodities: Rates, Rumors, and Facts," *New York Times* (March 3, 1980).
15. "St. Regis Corp., Target of Takeover Rumors, Says It Isn't for Sale," *Wall Street Journal* (June 28, 1984).
16. Koten, John, "GM-Toyota Talks on Small Car Venture Put Speculation Mills into High Gear," *Wall Street Journal* (August 3, 1982).
17. *Chicago Tribune* (June 1, 1984).
18. *Wall Street Journal* (September 13, 1984).
19. Antilla, Susan, "Business Is Always Good at the Wall Street Rumor Mill", *U.S.A. Today* (November 15, 1982).
20. "Big S&L in Hawaii Hit by Panic Withdrawls, 'Vicious Rumor Cited,'" *Wall Street Journal* (February 17, 1983).

Chapter Ten

WHAT CAN BE DONE ABOUT A RUMOR?

Option 1: Do Nothing

A company's first option is to ignore the rumor and hope that it will burn itself out. This "prudent" or "cautious" approach is a favorite among public relations people, among whom it is almost a tradition to feel that anti-rumor campaigns are dangerous and should be avoided except as a last resort.

To evaluate this option, however, one must find out what is going on and estimate the extent of the threat posed by the rumor. How much of a risk is the company taking by not doing something to quench a rumor? There are, indeed, times when putting out a small fire requires procedures more damaging than the fire itself. No one, for example, would want firemen to break down a door with axes and bring in a high-pressure hose to douse a wastebasket fire. Many public relations people likewise feel that some rumor-control tactics can be more damaging than the rumor itself. For example, the rumor that Tab contains 80 calories is something unwanted by the Coca-Cola Company but is not, in their opinion, worth launching any kind of rebuttal campaign.

One of the mains reasons for choosing not to do anything is the possibility that an anti-rumor campaign will call attention to the rumor itself. In Susan M. Goggins' survey at the University of Georgia concerning the McDonald's worm contamination rumor (see Chapter 8), 35 percent of the people interviewed heard the worm rumor only in connection with the McDonald's anti-rumor campaign policy of calling attention to the rumor's inaccuracy. One can argue that calling attention to a rumor through a media campaign rebuttal runs the risk of putting the story into wider circulation. There is also the risk of the "convergent rumor process," where calling attention to one rumor can make a company susceptible to other rumors.

Option 2: Do Something Locally

A second alternative is to deal with rumors locally as they erupt, somewhat like dealing with brush fires: Put each out as quickly and quietly as you can, then keep on the lookout for others. In all cases, however, treat each as a *local* problem. The procedure can be outlined as follows:

1. Find out as much as possible as soon as possible, and keep informed in terms of who is telling the rumor, why they are telling it, and where it is spreading. Information should be sought from company people in the field.

2. As soon as there is a reasonable picture of the situation, prepare instructions for company people who will be confronted by the rumors; they need to know what to do and what to say. Ask them to help gather information on the rumor and encourage them to be specific: From whom did they hear the rumor? How many people repeated it? Are there different versions of the rumor?

3. Have information handouts prepared for the company representatives and have refutations available to give people who report the rumor. The company's switchboard operators should record the frequency of inquiries. They should be told what they are supposed to say once they get the complete version of the story. Their responses must, of course, be much briefer and to the point than those of field people, who are likely to have extensive dialogue with the public about the rumor—for example, "Have you heard anything about this product?" and "If so, what?" This approach is probably the best single way of gauging the extent and the location of a rumor problem.

4. It is important to ascertain whether opinion-leaders representing special interest groups are involved. If so, find out

what the groups' goals are and what they see as obstacles. One should look for any orientation that will explain their motivation in the rumor process.

5. Information handouts should be prepared for such agencies as the Better Business Bureau in the area affected, as well as for newspapers and electronic media. It is well to explain that the handouts are not necessarily for broadcast but are being provided in case there are inquiries, such as letters, or people calling in for information.

6. If it turns out that the rumor is being generated through special populations in an area, it might be well to consider sending out letters regarding the rumor to opinion-leaders of these groups. Both Procter & Gamble and Entenmann's Bakery sent letters to religious leaders in the areas where they were being plagued by rumors concerning the ownership of their corporations. This action can be taken while still keeping the rumor problem localized.

7. Local representatives such as district managers and people in charge of public relations for particular territories can be given the option of having their own local press releases or media interviews if the situation becomes especially critical.

Option 3: Do Something—but Discreetly

Another approach is to deal with the rumor obliquely. It may be that company management recognizes the widespread threat of the rumor and wants to do something about it, but does not want to talk about it specifically as a rumor problem. The negative content of the rumor message is never mentioned; in fact, the rumor itself is never mentioned. This approach involves, for the most part, a public relations campaign focused on the opposite side of the content of the rumor message. This tack was taken by some of the oil companies during the oil crisis. Instead of actually rebutting the rumor's allegations of contrived shortages, high prices, and greedy motivations, they ran public relations campaigns about all the positive and constructive things oil companies were trying to do. In sum, this approach is a compromise in which it can be said that one is doing something about the rumor without being committed to going directly all out against it.

Option 4: Do Something All Out

A fourth strategy is to confront the rumor directly by going to the public with a refutation, using all the media resources available:

1. A press conference in which the allegation is stated and the denial is spelled out in a clear and convincing manner will reveal the rumor as blatantly untrue and also a grossly unfair occurrence.

2. It is vital to obtain as much exposure in the news as possible. News stories refuting a rumor are more convincing than paid advertisements. Have company spokesmen available for television and radio interviews. Indeed, rumors seem to be popular news items, and including a rumor expert as part of a presentation makes it more newsworthy. This approach helps to obtain media coverage because it is dealing with rumor as a phenomenon rather than as *your* rumor. Also, a public that learns about the nature of the rumor process is less likely to participate in it.

3. Advertising can be made more effective by including messages from credible people outside the company. Comments about the untruth and the injustice of the rumor by religious, civic, and media leaders lend credibility to paid time and/or space advertisements.

4. An anti-rumor campaign can sometimes be injected into the news through other events. Sometimes booster clubs or employee rallies can be used. Another effective technique is to threaten or actually bring lawsuits against rumor perpetrators. There may be no need to take the matter to court, but an impending suit will get the anti-rumor campaign into the news in its own right. It will also convince the public that the company means business about this "outrage."

Some Expert Advice[1]

Between sessions of a conference I attended at the London School of Economics, I was scanning a bulletin board in the dormitory recreation room. Under a notice titled "Emergencies" was another card headed "Fire Instructions," under which was the advisory, "In case of fire, try to put it out." I feel the same way about rumors. Either a rumor is a problem or it isn't. If it is ... *don't* spray around the edges. Don't merely hope it will simmer down. PUT IT OUT!!

- Don't use letters to groups, leaders, distinguished citizens, or others as a sole response.
- Don't hire detectives to try to "track down" a rumor, for the source is elusive. Even if it were found, the rumor will already have achieved an existence of its own.
- Don't rely *only* on spokespeople to meet with groups to talk in the company's behalf.

It is not that any of the above-mentioned actions will hurt anything; it is just that they take *time*. And if the rumor is really a problem—*Time is the worst enemy.*

One's single most important aim should be to end the rumor forcefully, as completely and as soon as possible. There appears to be a general, almost mystical reluctance on the part of some public relations people to confront a rumor problem directly, on the premise that public refutation of a rumor may call attention to it and make it more widespread than before. In sum, there seems to be a lurking fear that an open campaign will "add fuel to the fire."

Communications specialist Walter St. John gives seven ways to combat rumors in the book, *This is PR: The Realities of Public Relations.*[2] In conclusion he says, "Avoid referring to the rumor in disseminating the truth. (You don't want to reinforce the rumor itself ...)"[3]

In an article entitled, "Heed Rumors for Their Meaning," Robert Hershey says that "the best way to debunk a rumor is by presenting fact upon fact about the topic rather than trying to disprove the logic of the rumor. An official denial alone will never bedunk a rumor.[4]

A piece about rumor from the Royal Bank of Canada's monthly newsletter (reprinted in *Public Relations Journal*) supports the "speak no evil" position by saying, "As for our own part in spreading rumor, it is probably wise counsel to speak only what is necessary and in few words when the conversation gets around to rumor-prone matters."[5]

The idea of "residue effect," calling attention to a rumor by denying it, seems at first to make sense. The experiment cited in Chapter 8 demonstrates that direct denial of a statement about McDonald's hamburgers containing worms resulted in the same degree of negative feelings toward McDonald's as did the statement alone without the refutation.[6] However, it was also pointed out that the laboratory statement-refutation, followed immediately by an evaluation of the target, is not the same thing as a mass media refutation of a negative message. Following are two good examples of worst case scenarios in which successful mass media campaigns countered very ugly messages.

Toward the end of June 1967, a woman in Chicago died from a botulinus which was traced to some homemade gefilte fish prepared by someone for her family. Soon the contaminated fish became associated with Mother's Food Products[7] and that company was proclaimed as the source of the poison via newspapers and television. When the Chicago Health Department announced that it was possible that Mother's was the cause, public reaction was immediate—a barrage of mail and phone calls. The next day, however, Chicago and Federal health authorities said that Mother's was clear of any connection with the poisoning, and a release was sent out to all media announcing this fact. Members of the advertising staff of Solow/Wexton, Inc. called electronic media and news editors in New York and briefed them. They personally conveyed their own press releases because time was considered important. They bought full-page ads in New York and Chicago newspapers as well as in a number of religious publications. The point of the ad was that the "talk about Mother's gefilte fish was wrong. Mother's gefilte fish is fine today. It was fine yesterday. It will be fine tomorrow, because we make it under the best, the most scientifically sanitary conditions."[8] Reprints of the ad were mailed to the food trade and distributors were given copies to hand out to all their customers. Adrian Price of Mother's Food Products later wrote that "within just a few days, the truth had been presented to an important segment of our public. Fortunately things quickly settled back to normal."[9]

Another example of a dramatic refutation of a negative message involved Hygrade Food Products, a firm located outside Detroit. The company packages meat products, primarily hot dogs; their Ball Park Franks are the leading brand in the Detroit area, and the second biggest seller in the country.[10] In the latter part of October 1982, Operations Vice President Charles Ledgerwood heard that a woman in Detroit claimed to have found a piece of a razor blade in a Ball Park Frank. He met with the woman and believed her story. Later that day he met with the president of the company. They decided that "they would be open to the press, a course that seemed to offer the only chance of maintaining any public confidence."[11] Meanwhile the *Detroit News* ran a story under the heading, "Razor Blade Found in Hot Dog."[12] Television news programs made this their lead story, and more claims of finding objects in franks were made. All outstanding packages were called in, and that weekend all franks on hand (some one million pounds of them) were inspected with metal detectors.[13]

In the midst of this activity, facts began to come to light, revealing the claims as hoaxes. According to the dates on many of the packages, the metal items said to have been found in them should have shown signs of corrosion, but they did not. One woman confessed that she had lied; other complainants failed to show up for interviews with the police. The metal detectors found nothing.[14] Hygrade was not ready for a media blitz. Print advertising ran under the headline, "To our Ball Park Frank customers, thank you for bearing with us." The rest of the copy pointed out that "there was no evidence that any individual was ever in danger," that all products tested were shown to be safe, and that the franks were going back on the counters. Ads on television and radio announcements said the same thing.[15] Finally, the media also ran stories of the hoax as news. By March, sales in Detroit were ahead of where they had been before the episode.[16]

In a recent article on corporate rumors, the authors advise a media campaign as a "last resort." They say, "If all else fails, call a press conference in order to get out the facts. (But remember: once the media have the information, you no longer have control over who hears the rumor and the facts.)"[17] I disagree. One cannot afford to wait until "all else fails." The reasoning that more people will hear a rumor as the result of a media campaign is simply not logical. Hearing a damaging allegation as a rumor is one kind of social-psychological phenomenon; encountering a news item about a *false* rumor being circulated by misinformed and misled transmitters is a very different phenomenon.

Once the story of a false rumor has been released to the media, the "rumor" becomes "news." News has different dynamics than rumors, and the difference is in the victim's favor. The above-cited caveat about losing control of a rumor "once the media have the information" misses the point. What kind of control does one have over a rumor *before* any public information campaign? "News" about a false rumor is transmitted via different structures than the rumor networks we discussed previously. Also, a message that is *news* loses the capacity to be transmitted as a *rumor*, since the whole driving force and motivation for telling a rumor will be defused: It is, indeed, no longer a substitute for news, and it is no longer entertainment or diversion. The most important point is that people pass on rumors to other persons or instigate a rumor into a network because they are isolates ... unpopular, lonely people or individuals trying to get attention, recognition, or some kind of response by relating a story that has sensational value. When a rumor becomes news, it is shared by a whole population, and relating it does not produce the same sensational reaction. In short, the attraction of telling a story can be eliminated by a media campaign which defuses it. A media campaign can reduce the attractiveness of telling a story even more if it makes the rumor look ridiculous. Most people will refrain from telling a rumor if the response they anticipate is ridicule.

Despite all the misgivings that have been aired, I have never heard of a media confrontation campaign against a commercial rumor that has "backfired" or had any other serious undesirable consequences. On the other hand, direct confrontation campaigns such as those carried out by Mother's Food Products, General Foods, Entenmann's Bakery, Stroh Beer, Church's Fried Chicken, and John Gibbon's Restaurant were all successful. The only major difficulty that can arise is failure of the media campaign to reach the participating population. In this regard, I suspect that a problem with the Bubble Yum campaign was that school children seldom read *New York Times* advertising.

Prevention Where Possible

There is no 100 percent effective technique for preventing rumors. The best approach is to maintain goodwill and positive public reactions on an ongoing basis. It is wise to have as few people as possible with hostile motivations towards the organization. The bigger and more successful a company, the more vulnerable it is as a target for sensational rumors, simply because many people resent big and successful companies. Accordingly, the bigger and more successful a company, the greater the effort it should make to maintain a positive public image. Personnel who meet the public should be trained to maintain friendly relations. There should be a well-thought-out procedure for dealing with complaints, and everyone should know about a company's charitable efforts and public service programs.

Another action that may help to reduce the number and virility of rumors in the marketplace is dissemination of public information about the nature of rumors. Studies in persuasion have shown that trying to change a person's attitude by presenting refutational information is not as effective as combining the argument with a psychological explanation for why people hold the position they do. Research reported by Katz and his colleagues[18] indicated that information about racial equality alone did not modify subjects' attitudes towards minorities as much as "the facts" accompanied by a brief explanation on the dynamics of prejudice—that is, the reason some people hold negative views toward minority groups.

People who understand the dynamics and motivations of the rumor process are far less likely to become involved in irresponsible and destructive hearsay and more likely to develop a critical mindset toward rumors. If people learn to be critical of the content of any message and to question the motivations of a message-bearer, they are less likely to be a listener and transmitter of false stories. And, indeed, bringing about that understanding has been the objective of this book.

Synopsis of Recommended Steps in Rumor Control

A. Alert Procedure
1. On first hearing a rumor, note the location and wording of the allegation and target.
2. Keep alert for any other rumors to see if the original report was spurious.
3. If rumors increase to ten or more, send requests to dis-

tributors, franchise managers, and whoever else meets
the public to find out who told the rumor to the person
reporting it. It is important to specify the regional bound-
aries of the problem and the characteristics of the participating population. Distribute forms that can be filled out
for the above information, as well as fact sheets rebutting
the rumor.

4. Check with competitors to see if they share the problem.
   Try to find out if the target has moved from your company to them or from them to yours, or if it has spread
   throughout the industry.

B. Evaluation
   1. Check for a drop in sales or a slowdown in sales increase.
   2. Monitor person-hours required to answer phone calls and
      mail.
   3. Keep tabs on the morale of the company personnel meet-
      ing people in the corporation. Do they feel harassed? Do
      they feel that management is doing enough to help them?
   4. Design a marketing survey to find out what percentage of
      the public believes any part of the rumor.
   5. Make an assessment of the threat or potential threat the
      rumor poses to profits. Is the corporation in danger of
      appearing to be an inept, impotent, and passive victim of
      the rumor problem? How much is management's image
      affected by the way things are going? The next move is a
      judgment call. If it seems that something more should be
      done, then it is time to move to the next square.

C. Launch a Media Campaign
   1. Assemble all facts about the extent of the problem to
      present to co-workers and superiors. Be prepared for
      resistance from people who support the myth that
      "pussyfooting is the best policy."
   2. Based on information gathered in the previous phases,
      decide on the geographical regions for implementing the
      campaign. If it is a local rumor, treat it locally; if it is a
      national rumor, treat it nationally.
   3. Based on information gathered in the previous phases,
      decide on the demographic features of the carrying popu-
      lation.
   4. Select appropriate media outlets and construct appropri-
      ate messages.

5. Decide on what points to refute. (Don't deny *more* than is in the allegation.) If the allegation is of the contamination variety, be careful not to bring up any offensive association or to trigger potential "residuals" in the refutation.
6. Two important points to make in any campaign are that the allegations are *untrue* and *unjust.* It should be implied that the company's business is not suffering, but that "what's right is right!" and that people who pass on the rumor are "going against the American sense of fair play!"
7. Line up spokespeople such as scientists, civic and/or religious leaders, rumor experts—whoever you think appropriate—to make statements on the company's behalf.

If all the above is done properly, the problem is well on the way to being solved.

Endnotes

1. Koenig, Fredrick, "Combatting Rumor: The Direct Approach," unpublished manuscript.
2. St. John, Walter, in Doug Newsome and Alan Scott (Eds.), *This is PR: The Realities of Public Relations* (Belmont, California: Wadsworth Publishing Co., 1975), pp. 192-194.
3. St. John, Walter, *op. cit.*
4. Hershey, Robert, "Heed Rumors for Their Meaning," *Personnel Journal* 34 (1956), p. 301.
5. "Rumor, False Report, and Propaganda," *Public Relations Journal* 13 (July, 1957), p. 23.
6. Tybout, Alice, Bobby Calder, and Brian Sternthal, "Using Information Processing Theory to Design Marketing Strategies," *Journal of Marketing Research*, Vol. 18 (February 1981), pp. 73-97.
7. Price, Adrian, "Mother's Counters All That Talk With Some Emergency Public Relations," *Public Relations Journal* (October 23, 1967), p. 44.
8. Price, Adrian, *op. cit.*
9. Price, Adrian, *op. cit.*
10. Colvin, Geoffrey, "Lessons from a Hot Dog Maker's Ordeal," *Fortune* (March 7, 1983), pp. 77-82.
11. Colvin, Geoffrey, *op. cit.*, p. 78.
12. Colvin, Geoffrey, *op. cit.*, p. 82.
13. McKinsey, Kitty, "Hot Dogs and Sympathy," *Detroit Free Press* (February 27, 1983), p. 10.
14. Colvin, Geoffrey, *op. cit.*, p. 82.
15. Courter, Eileen, "Reputation, PR Helped Hygrade Survive Hot Dog

Hoax," *Adweek* (April 4, 1983), p. 43.

16. Colvin, Geoffrey, *op. cit.*, p. 82.

17. Esposito, J.L., and R.L. Rosnow, "Corporate Rumors: How They Start and How To Stop Them," *Management Review* 72 (April 1983), p. 45.

18. Katz, Daniel, Ivan Sarnoff, and Charles M. Clintock, "Ego-Defense and Attitude Change," *Human Relations* 9 (1956), pp. 27-45.

INDEX

DATE DUE

FEB 28 1991			